PLEASE RETURN TO
W. 868 337 6650

Sandra —
May you live w...
Love,
Julie
2/2023

The SNAP method is brilliant. In one simple practice, Julie Potiker integrates brain science, mindfulness, compassion, and other effective tools for lifting your mood, easing anxiety, calming stress, and opening your heart. Full of practical wisdom, she leads readers through funny stories, tender care, and many different applications of the SNAP method. Throughout, she is a super-smart, encouraging, and hopeful friend. A wonderful book!

Rick Hanson, Ph.D., author of *Resilient: How to Grow an Unshakable Core of Calm, Strength, and Happiness*

"Life is rarely as easy as a snap, but Julie Potiker finds a relatable way of helping you contend with the most challenging experiences of life by using her clever and easy SNAP method. Tapping into our natural capacity for healing and ease, and building on solid science, Julie leads the reader by the hand with her own brand of humor, warmth and humility into a place of greater wellbeing and joy. Super accessible and incredibly practical, this book will become your best friend in times of need."

Steven Hickman, PsyD
Licensed Clinical Psychologist
Executive Director, Center for Mindful Self-Compassion
Founding Director, UC San Diego Center for Mindfulness

This book is a handy resource for managing difficult emotions based on the elegant acronym, SNAP. The author, Julie Potiker, generously shares her personal experiences, and even a few poems, to illustrate how mindfulness and self-compassion can help us cope with life's challenges. Rest assured, help is just a snap away!

Christopher Germer, PhD
Lecturer (Part-time), Harvard Medical School
Co-developer, *Mindful Self-Compassion* training
Author, *The Mindful Path to Self-Compassion*

"This book is a treasure box of practices for nearly any difficult moment you might find yourself in. All variations on the simple yet profound Soothing, Naming, Acting, Praising SNAP! practice developed by the author, each chapter provides examples of how, why, and when you can apply this method to rebalance when you are feeling thrown off. In her authentic, honest, and heartfelt voice, Julie Potiker brings the material to life by sharing how she's applied the practice of SNAP to real-world situations ranging from annoying to crushing. What a gift! I'm off to put sticky notes in my home, car, and workplace to remind me to SNAP…"

Cassandra Vieten, PhD, Director of Research at the Arthur C Clarke Center for Human Imagination at the University of California, San Diego; Executive Director, John W. Brick Mental Health Foundation, and author of Mindful Motherhood.

This book is a delight to read. It's filled with science backed techniques, but you wouldn't know it with Julie Potiker's engaging, humorous, and humble style. I found myself both laughing out loud and with eyes brimming with tears as I followed Julie through her adventures using her clever and effective SNAP method to meet the myriad of challenges that have arisen in her life- as they do for each of us. This book is as entertaining and inspiring as it is helpful. Above all, it is a guide for how build a life when life feels stacked against you. One SNAP at a time.

Michelle Becker, M.A., LMFT
Founder of Wise Compassion
Developer of Compassion for Couples training
Co-founder, Mindful Self-Compassion Teacher Training
Senior Trainer and Mentor, UCSD Center for Mindfulness

"In this book, Julie Potiker weaves together stories from her own life with poetry and life tips to show how meditation practice can be easy as snap! Whether you are plagued with anxiety, overwhelmed with challenging current events, or simply having a bad day, this easy-to-remember acronym can help remind you to be kind and supportive to yourself – to treat yourself as you would treat a good friend."

Karen Bluth, PhD, Department of Psychiatry, University of North Carolina-Chapel Hill, Author, *The Self-Compassion Workbook for Teens, The Self-Compassionate Teen, Mindfulness and Self-Compassion for Teen ADHD, Self-Compassion for Girls: A Guide for Parents, Teachers, and Coaches*

Julie combines rich storytelling, compelling science, heartfelt poetry, and her clever SNAP acronym to help us manage life's stressors and curveballs. Whether you're managing grief, parenting, or just doing your best to live in this challenging world, you can lean on SNAP to support and soothe your body, mind, and heart.

Sara J. Schairer *(pronouns: she/her/hers)*
Founder, Exec. Dir.
Compassion It
858-349-9245

SNAP!
FROM CHAOS TO CALM

JULIE POTIKER

ARCHWAY
PUBLISHING

Archway Publishing books may be ordered through booksellers or by contacting:

Archway Publishing
1663 Liberty Drive
Bloomington, IN 47403
www.archwaypublishing.com
844-669-3957

Because of the dynamic nature of the Internet, any web addresses or
links contained in this book may have changed since publication and
may no longer be valid. The views expressed in this work are solely those
of the author and do not necessarily reflect the views of the publisher,
and the publisher hereby disclaims any responsibility for them.

Any people depicted in stock imagery provided by Getty Images are
models, and such images are being used for illustrative purposes only.
Certain stock imagery © Getty Images.

ISBN: 978-1-6657-3192-8 (sc)
ISBN: 978-1-6657-3190-4 (hc)
ISBN: 978-1-6657-3191-1 (e)

Library of Congress Control Number: 2022919169

Print information available on the last page.

Archway Publishing rev. date: 12/16/2022

CONTENTS

CONTENTS

INTRODUCTION

Everyone has their metaphorical bag of rocks they carry through life. My rocks are not the same as yours, and through the years, the rocks change in shape and size. Sometimes the bag is so heavy, I fear it will topple me. Other times, it feels like it is half-filled with polished pebbles. This journey through life has been made easier by a path that I found in 2010 when I was a student in a new class called Mindful Self-Compassion at University of California at San Diego (UCSD) taught by Steve Hickman, PsyD, and Michelle Becker, LMFT.

Since 2014 I have had the pleasure of teaching Mindful Self-Compassion (MSC), which was created by Christopher Germer, PhD, a leader in the integration of mindfulness, compassion, and psychotherapy, and Kristin Neff, PhD, a pioneering researcher in the field of self-compassion. I love the curriculum, and I am especially grateful for and connected with our tribe of MSC teachers spread across the planet. I have also had the good fortune to learn from Rick Hanson, PhD, who has guided my learning and my teaching with "Taking in the Good"—experience-dependent neuroplasticity training. It has been a privilege and a pleasure to help people manage their lives with less suffering and more ease by teaching them evidence-based techniques to manage difficult emotions, thereby rewiring their brain for happiness and resilience.

I'm one of those people that walks my talk. I try different teachings all the time, and when I find one that works for me, I fold it into my life and my teaching. For years I taught this cool acronym, RAIN, created by Michele McDonald and widely popularized by the wonderful Tara Brach. RAIN stands for recognize, allow, investigate and non-identification: recognize that you are having the emotion; allow the emotion to be there so you can work with it; investigate why it is happening, with compassion and without judgment; and do not identify, meaning do not run away or spin out on the story line. Years later the N is now taught as *Nourish*, which is a nod to all the great benefits of having a self-compassion practice. I teach RAIN in my first book, *Life Falls Apart, But You Don't Have To: Mindful Methods for Staying Calm in the Midst of Chaos,* as well as all the other mindfulness and mindful self-compassion tools that make up my big beautiful toolbox, helping me to lighten the load of the rocks that I carry.

Now I'm thrilled to introduce SNAP, a new system I created, that works better for me than RAIN because it front-loads self-compassion by starting with soothing touch, a practice named and taught in the MSC course. I also love that it has a somatic component—the snap of my fingers—and dance-like moves with my hands and arms to accompany the acronym when I teach it. The fingers snap, **Soothing touch**: the hands go to your body for a release of calming oxytocin and endorphins. Your hands can move palms down as you **Name the emotion**, name it to tame it—the prefrontal cortex calms the nervous system further, creating some space between the feeling and you. Then your arms extend as you **Act**, choosing whatever technique is available to you from your mindfulness toolbox to help you change your channel. Finally, bringing your hands into prayer hands at your heart, **Praise** allows you to move into gratitude for yourself, your practice, the universe, or your deity of choice. I think the hand movements help to remember the practice; but either way, I imagine if you can remember to snap your fingers, you can remember SNAP when you want to snap out of chaos and into calmness.

Sometimes in the liminal space between sleeping and waking, I have flashes of insight. That is how SNAP was born. I started teaching it, and blogged about it right away, and I have found that my students are remembering to use it when they feel activated by a difficult emotion. I'm hoping that teachers start teaching it and that a wave of healing begins with a snap of the fingers!

As you read through the stories in the book, you will see how SNAP can be used for everything that life throws at you. The Act element will differ—meaning the tool you choose from your mindfulness toolbox—based on what is available to you and what you need in that moment.

This is a smaller book than *Life Falls Apart, But You Don't Have To* because I'm writing it to push the practice of SNAP out into the world. If you feel like this book plopped you onto the middle of the path and you could use more foundation in the concepts, please skim through *Life Falls Apart, But You Don't Have To*. You can purchase it on Kindle for $3.49, Kindle unlimited for free, and in paperback for $12.99 on Amazon. I hope to have an audible version ready by the time *SNAP!* is in your hands!

As you practice SNAP, you might find that it works better for some issues than others. Or maybe it works some days better than others. My hope is that with practice it becomes second nature, helping your boulders become rocks and your rocks become pebbles. Who knows, maybe someday the pebbles will become sand and float away with the tide.

I organized this book by general topic headings to help readers find what might be helpful quickly. SNAP works for everything, but if you have a parenting issue, it might be helpful to read the chapter with parenting stories instead of the chapter on grief.

Please enjoy skipping around in this book, looking for what might be helpful to lighten your unique load in the moment. I welcome your feedback and questions. You can find me at www. MindfulMethodsForLife.com. If you are interested in deepening your practice by listening to guided meditations, my free podcast, *Balanced Mind with Julie Potiker*, has oodles to choose from that may assist you in moving out of emotional chaos and into a state of calmness.

CAROUSEL IN HELL

There's no jumping off this carousel in hell;
Life has glued my aged hands to the pole;
My mind departs.

Dropping to the earth,
I notice with alarm that I am no longer solid,
A pile of bone fragments and ash—no body to make my
escape.

I must wait until a forceful enough wind picks me up and
moves me.
I wish to be blown to the ocean,
The sea spreading me far and wide on the underwater
highway.

I could settle there, joining a coral reef,
A haven for brightly colored and delicate fish.
I see butterfly fish, parrot fish, and those fish that look like
soft triangles, with the thin curved white piece floating
behind them—can't think of their name and they are my
favorite—oh, moorish idols!

It's peaceful and beautiful here.
I stay as long as I can, knowing that because I'm still alive,
I must eventually teleport my mind back to my body,
stuck on the bloody merry-go-round on land.
Decisions must be made,
Boundaries must be held,
I stay in the sea as long as I can.

SNAP FOR ANGER

I t's normal and appropriate to feel anger, but getting back to baseline, where you feel safe and settled, is the goal for mental health and well-being. Anger causes stress in your body, and too much stress can cause problems all over your body. A study in the journal *Psychoneuroendocrinology* linked stress hormones with higher blood sugar in type 2 diabetes. [Note: "The longitudinal association of changes in diurnal cortisol features with fasting glucose: MESA," *Psychoneuroendocrinology*, 2020, 104698.] There are multitudes of scientific studies illustrating the relationship between stress and negative health outcomes. They all have one thing in common, showing how cortisol, the stress hormone, wreaks havoc on us! We need cortisol and adrenaline to support our ability to fight, flight, and freeze. But when the danger is over, we need to be able to calm our nervous systems, soothe ourselves, and allow ourselves to move back into the safety zone.

WORDS THAT HURT AND MAD SKILLS

When I was a little kid, I used to think that words said in anger were a true reflection of the thoughts and feelings of the monster doing the screaming. The insults stuck with me. It wasn't until adulthood that I changed that narrative. I learned that sometimes humans reach a boiling point and toxic hot lava comes shooting out of their mouths without them controlling the content of their poisonous rant. Worse still, often they have no memory of their verbal diarrhea.

With therapy, my meditation, self-compassion practice, and time, I eventually forgave my mom for all the horrendous things she said when she had one of her episodes. I know she loved me to pieces and respected me. I still can't erase the one doozey though: "If you were still a practicing attorney, I could respect you!" she shouted at me as I gathered up my infant son and got the hell away from her. Luckily, she had twenty-five years after that fateful day to illustrate that the statement wasn't true. I was also fortunate to be married to a man who wouldn't let me become estranged from my parents. I have a scar there, but it's more like a faded memory.

We carry these scars into our marriages and our parenting. I bent over backward (still do) to never let anger out in an uncontrolled way at my kids. The problem with stuffing anger deeper, though, is that it grows bigger and darker. What we resist persists. What we can feel, we can heal. It was much healthier for my mom to pop off and let out her rage than keeping it in. It was unfortunate for her target, but she got the poison out of her body. In my case, since I am so uncomfortable with anger from being traumatized

by it as a child, unexpressed anger can cause depression if I am
not vigilant in my self-compassion practice.

LET'S SNAP ANGER

Soothing touch: Place your hand over your heart. Oxytocin and
endorphins will release, helping your nervous system calm down.
This is the coolest thing ever—that we can use the mammalian
caregiver response, which evolved to keep infants safe, on ourselves
to calm our nervous system! When an infant cries and is cuddled
and soothed by a caregiver, a cascade of feel-good hormones
(including oxytocin) and endorphins get released in the infant
and the caregiver! This counteracts the threat-defense system
that Paul Gilbert, the creator of Compassion-Focused Therapy,
explains happens when we criticize ourselves: the primitive part
of our brains, the amygdala, gets triggered and releases cortisol
and adrenaline to get us ready to fight, flight, or freeze. [Note:
Dacher Keltner, "Hands On Research: The Science of Touch,
Greater Good Science Center," September 29, 2010.]

Name the emotion: Label the emotion. "I am having anger."
Locate it in your body. The mere act of labeling the emotion helps
you to step back from it.

Act: Apply the appropriate mindful method. Start with positive self-talk, like calling yourself "sweetheart," and acknowledge that what happened was hard. If you notice a constriction somewhere in your body, try to imagine softening the area and relaxing into the space around it. Send healing energy or light into the space.

Praise: Send healing thoughts to yourself, like "Julie, I love you. You'll get through this." or "It's tough to feel this way, but you are not alone." When your mind is occupied with sending healing thoughts to your body, it cannot be in a recursive loop of negative thoughts. Your brain can't spin out a story line of anger and hurt while giving yourself love.

When you feel a positive mental state, like the love is working, let it fill you up for a breath or two. With this simple act, you take advantage of positive neuroplasticity and rewire your brain for more happiness and resilience.

Along with SNAP, I also add more mindfulness meditation to my days and get more vitamin D by spending time outside. Together, these three things have helped me be in a space of healing my anger and the fear underneath.

If you're going through something similar and struggling with anger, know these tools can make a difference in your overall well-being. Acknowledge your anger and try to get beneath it to identify the softer emotion. You might find fear under the anger, and if you drop deeper, the need to be seen, heard, or loved. Our most basic human needs might not be being met. Then increase your mindfulness practices, such as keeping a gratitude journal or doing a few minutes of mindfulness meditation each day.

With practice, you get to a point where you flip into these methods without thinking. One day you will realize you are less reactive because you are automatically using your practice. It's funny. I always say I have mad skills! I never thought about the fact that they are *mad* skills, as in skills to manage anger! Thank goodness I can SNAP out of it!

2

SNAP FOR ANXIETY

MINDFUL METHODS FOR ANXIETY IN THE WORLD

I love the media headline to this study: "Study links rising stress, depression in US to pandemic-related losses and media consumption." Extensive exposure to pandemic-related news and conflicting information in the news are among the strongest predictors of pandemic-specific stress. Intuitively, we know this is true. We have been through an unfathomable few years together. We need to do whatever is in our power to help ourselves heal so we can heal our communities. [Note: "The unfolding COVID-19 pandemic: A probability-based nationally representative study of mental health in the United States," *Science Advances*, 2020, eabd5390.]

Chronic stress triggers inflammation in the body and the brain. The stress can cause symptoms body-wide, ranging from headaches, feelings of despair, anxiety, and anger, to memory and sleep problems. When I'm stressed out, I have trouble staying asleep and get all sorts of problems in my gut, from constipation to the other end of misery. Your skin my flair up and you may have discomfort in your muscles and joints. Moving down the body, your heart may palpitate (mine does), and you can have an increase in blood pressure and an increase risk of high cholesterol and heart attack. Moving now to your stomach, stress can cause nausea, stomach pain, heart burn, and weight gain. Stress in your pancreas may increase your risk of diabetes, and stress in your intestines may cause everything from constipation to diarrhea. In your reproductive system, it can cause lower sperm count, reduced libido, and impotence in men, and more painful periods and reduced sexual desire in women. Stress lowers your ability to fight or recover from illness. [Note: "Interleukin-1 receptor on hippocampal neurons drives social withdrawal and cognitive deficits after chronic social stress," *Molecular Psychiatry*, 2020.]

We all have areas of life that sometimes feel overwhelming, over the top, and just plain too much to handle. Add in a global health crisis, the latest political news, and social injustices, and it can feel like we're on the edge of a full-blown meltdown.

Regardless of which category of "storm clouds" has you veering out of alignment with your joy, clarity, and overall well-being, mindfulness is a wonderful tool for finding your way back to center.

Soothing touch: Give your body a head start in calming down. It taps into your body's mammalian caregiver response and releases oxytocin and opiates in your brain to counteract cortisol, the stress hormone.

Place your hands where you find it soothing. Practice placing your hands on your heart, your belly, cheeks, upper arms in a hug, or hold your own hands. See what placement comforts you most.

Name the emotion: That is, say, "I'm feeling frustrated. I feel upset. I feel scared. I feel angry." Labeling the emotion engages the thinking brain and calms your system down. Drop into the emotion and see what's there. Avoid judging it. Simply observe with curiosity. This is the heart of what mindfulness is all about. It takes practice, but soon you'll be able to tune in and notice what's happening inside you. Once you notice these feelings, you can work with them, giving yourself room to breathe and changing your relationship to them.

Act: Apply the appropriate mindful method tool to nourish yourself. Notice that you are physically safe right now, presuming you are. You have a roof over your head. And more than likely you are not in physical danger. Open up your senses. Notice what you see in your environment. Spend a few moments listening to whatever sounds are present. See how the air feels on your skin. Let yourself realize that you are actually safe.

Praise: What should you hear or do right now to make yourself feel better? Create a phrase and repeat it as a mantra to yourself.

I am healthy and strong.
I am safe.
I will get through this.
Whatever unfolds, I will be there to meet it.
I am loved and appreciated.

Focus on the mantra until it sinks in and you begin to believe it. Don't worry if it feels forced at first.

As a bonus, change the channel by popping in a positive mental state from a memory. Feel that goodness for a breath or two to transform it from a mental state to a neural trait. This will rewire your brain for more happiness and resilience.

Here are a few other action tips to try next time you feel anxiety rising inside of you.

Practice deep breathing. Take several deep breaths. Go longer on the exhale to calm the nervous system; try counting to four on the inhale and to six on the exhale.

Access mindfulness with a physical object. Focusing on an object helps shift the mind from worrying thoughts. Go exploring and choose a stone for this purpose. It doesn't have to be fancy; it just needs to feel nice in your palm and fit in your pocket. Anytime you feel anxious or stressed, reach for it, feel its texture, and focus on that physical object instead of your worries.

Focus on gratitude. You can't be grateful and worried simultaneously. Keep a gratitude journal. Write in it at least once a day, answering two questions: (1) What did I enjoy today? (2) What am I grateful for today?

Meditate. If you're not already a meditator, try it! It's easier than you think to jump right in, and it's great for managing anxiety. Try a free meditation app like Insight Timer (my favorite). Try the *Balanced Mind with Julie Potiker* podcast, also free and relaxing.

Mindfulness helps us pause and step back from overwhelming feelings. It provides a calming strategy for challenging moments and helps to SNAP us back into balance.

MORNING MIND FLOW

The first thing I notice is the sound.

A wall of high fidelity sound.
I fold myself into the pale turquoise cushion on the chair
and let it in.

There's twilling, tweeting, and something that sounds
like call-and-response singing, an octave above high C.

Underneath, or on top, of all that sound is the constant
gentle roar; yes, a roar, but sweet, of the river—sort of
like a white-noise machine; or maybe it's pink noise, or
brown noise.

I feel my palms and the underside of my fingers getting
hot, wrapped around my white ceramic mug with the
artist rendering of an elk, his antlers partially covered by
my thumbs.

The next thing to come online is my vision.

The bright green heart-shaped leaves of the aspen trees are
shimmering and quaking on their delicate stems.
Bugs, flying things, butterflies, and bees are flitting
around in the sunlight slanting through the shadows of
the trees.

I rest my mug on the arm of the chair and pull my cozy flannel pajama top around me in a hug.

The thin, bamboo, hot-flash-preventing nightgown isn't enough to keep off the chill of an Idaho summer morning. My fleece-lined slippers enclose my feet as I notice where the fresh, cool air is making contact with my skin.

I'm reminded of summer camp: cool mornings in the upper peninsula of Michigan; using a rake to make patterns in the dirt in front of our cabin at Interlochen National Music Camp; red knee socks pulled all the way up to my worn navy-corduroy knickers (pants that button below the knee, not underwear, for my UK friends!); hoping to win the best cabin award each week.

My mind back now to the present: a carpenter ant running across the rough stones. How does he move so fast?

There must be some small animal in the eaves, because there are crumpled dry leaves and stems arranged haphazardly on the stones below the roof, right next to the sliding doors to the breakfast room. Perhaps a soft, furry little houseguest is joining me for breakfast while I enjoy my coffee in her world.

MINDFUL METHODS FOR MEDICAL ANXIETY

There are so many situations that cause anxiety, with medical issues ranking near the top of the list. The beauty of SNAP is that you tailor it to the situation. The S (soothing touch) and the N (name the emotion) will be consistent, but the A is where variation comes in as you see what tool fits to help you in the moment. The P (praise) is usually the same for me—feeling gratitude for my practice, my teachers, my life. Below is a story of using mindfulness-grounding tools from my toolbox (the A in SNAP) for anxiety that I was feeling in anticipation of a medical procedure.

MINDFULNESS IN THE CAT SCAN MACHINE

"Oh, you have a stone?" he asked.

"Yes, it's a here-and-now stone—a kind of a meditation thing. Is it OK if I hold it in my hand during the procedure? I mean, can I take it in the CAT scan machine?"

"Sure, I don't see why not," he said. This lab tech has probably seen it all.

"I think you might be a little dehydrated. Have you had much to drink today?"

"Your people just gave me a liter of that 'water,' so I've had that and a couple of cups of tea," I replied, trying to stay in touch with my breathing to quell the anxiety coming up in my body as he was tapping the veins on the inside of my arm, below my elbow.

"The stuff you drank has contrast dye material in it, and it's dehydrating. And I'm thinking you might have come in a little dehydrated, because your veins feel a little flat."

"Ugh. Do you want to try the other arm? I just had blood taken from the other arm thirty minutes ago, but you might find a better vein there ..."

"No, this arm will be OK. It's going to be a little more painful because I have to put a catheter in the vein, not just a needle," he explained while digging into my arm.

"Wow! That really hurts!" I'm breathing, I'm breathing, I'm breathing.

"OK. Place both arms up over your head. The machine will tell you when to hold your breath, and when to release your breath. We will do two rounds, and then I'll let you know when the dye from the IV will go in. You might feel sensations, like you will pee, but that will only last a minute. I'll be behind the wall, but if you need anything, speak loudly and I will hear you."

"May I be safe, may I be happy, may I be healthy, may I live with ease ... may I be safe, may I be happy, may I be healthy, may I live with ease ..." Round and round I whispered these phrases out loud, only stopping when the machine voice said to hold my breath.

"OK, here comes the IV contrast dye," he said.

At that point I felt for the little ridges and cracks in my here-and-now stone, moving it around in my left hand, my hand cupped open above my head, the back of my hand resting on the pillow.

I then counted my breaths.

At about the number ten, I felt the sensation of the dye slowly washing up the inside of my body. It was warm and heavy. I wondered whether I had let go of some urine on the table, and I hoped I had not. The heavy feeling traveled up my trunk, pressing my shoulders, head, and neck into the table. And by the time I hit number thirty, the sensations had vanished.

"OK, all done!" he said as he stepped back into the room and unwrapped the inside of my right elbow.

"Wow, that was really weird. I think I'm going to write about it."

"It is really weird," he replied. "But it's perfectly normal for contrast dye. Make sure you drink two liters of water in the next two hours to clear all the contrast material out of your body."

I left the building with a Buddha belly, wondering how I would stuff more liquid into my bloated frame. I was freezing. It must have been in the low 60s in the room with the machine, and there was a fan blowing the arctic air on my head during the procedure. I could wear my yoga pants, tank, and Smartwool base layer, but not my sweatshirt. He even let me keep my shoes on.

My husband decided soup was in order! Soup broth would count for some of the fluid I was supposed to pour into myself, and hot herbal tea would make up the balance, all the while doing the job of warming me up from the inside out.

In less than four hours, a radiologist evaluated the scan, and I got the fabulous news from my internal medicine doctor that the report was "unremarkable."

What is remarkable is the technology!

In a procedure that lasted less than fifteen minutes, they saw inside my body from my neck to my hips and determined that my organs, vessels, lymph nodes, bones, and soft tissue were normal.

That is the gift I was hoping for, and my mindful methods practice allowed me to stay present for the present. I wasn't imagining the worst, but the relief I felt made me aware that deep down inside there had been a little nugget of fear. Life is so fragile. Nothing is guaranteed.

I've been working on the practice of embracing impermanence. It's a difficult concept—to feel relaxed and calm with your own mortality. I'd like more time here on the planet, to love and teach love. I have many places yet to travel. I imagine having much more joy and heartbreak in the years to come.

But I know that I can only control what I can control: my diet, exercise, and attitude.

The attitude part means I can control how I treat my fellow sentient beings on the planet. I can try to be kind, to withhold judgment from others and myself. I can try to pause so I may make a more skillful response instead of a knee-jerk reaction.

I'm grateful that, for now, I've been given a reprieve to continue the practice of being the change I want to see in the world.

The SNAP in this story was heavy on applying appropriate mindful method tools.

Soothing touch: If you cannot place your hand on your body (I couldn't put my hand on my heart in the CAT scan machine), then imagine putting it over your heart or where you find it soothing.

Name the emotion: Just naming the emotion as anxiety will help you feel less out of control.

Act: Breathing techniques, longer on the exhale or counting your breaths as a meditation, can be done even in the throes of fear. A here-and-now stone to ground yourself is especially helpful, as it gives you a tactile cue to relax.

Praise: Congratulate yourself for using your power. Allow yourself to marinate in your good choices. Thank yourself for applying the tools.

How wonderful that we can SNAP anxiety!

MINDFULNESS FOR CONTAGIOUS ANXIETY

We all know what it feels like to be going about our business and then be emotionally blindsided by someone in a state of anxiety, anger, or unrest. Even if we were feeling all right before that, it's challenging to leave those disturbing interactions without absorbing some of those emotions ourselves. On the flip side, though, we can be having a crappy day and then find ourselves around people who are loving and kind and happy, and it lifts us up.

I was in the emergency room with my daughter recently, and she and the doctor just didn't jibe. Their energies didn't match up, and they weren't a good fit. His bedside manner wasn't compassionate or empathetic, and she became defensive and angry.

At one point he came into the room and said, "I can feel your displeasure all the way out in the hallway."

At the time I thought, *Wow ... what a f—k! Keep it to yourself! That's not helpful!* I share it with you now as a perfect example of how anger and anxiety can spread like wildfire once it's present.

In fact, in a study published in *Nature Neuroscience* in 2018, a group of scientists did an experiment to see if they could prove anxiety is contagious. They took pairs of mice and exposed one to a mild form of stress before returning it to be with the other unstressed mouse. They discovered that the formerly unstressed mouse became stressed when exposed to the stressed mouse.

So, bad news, folks: anxiety is contagious; but fortunately, so is happiness. To be more responsible social citizens, we can all focus on spreading more happiness than anxiety in the world, and mindfulness is a great way to do it.

SNAP FOR CONTAGIOUS ANXIETY

Soothing touch: Place your hand where it is helpful. If it seems like putting your hand on your body might be awkward or make the situation worse, just put your hands inside each other.

Name the emotion: Anxiety! Then you might gently inquire why you feel this way. Whether you're responding to everyday frustrations or large-scale, upsetting world events, your feelings are valid. You're having a moment, and that's real.

Act: What do I really need to hear right now? What would make me feel better? Answer these questions, then give that to yourself. For example, "You're strong." "You'll get through it." "This too shall pass." Whatever trope you want to say to yourself will actually make you feel better. Use it!

Praise: Push a positive mental state into your mind, let it land, and create a positive neural trait. If you're able to shift yourself into a more positive state of mind, you'll benefit not only your own mind and body, but also those of everyone you encounter.

How cool is that?

SNAP FOR EQUANIMITY

I think about equanimity as if my body is rooted in the ground, long strong tendrils reaching through the soil into the earth. My roots are drinking nutrients from below and nourishing my trunk, branches, and leaves. The sun is coming down from above and making the magic of photosynthesis occur. In the understory, below the surface, the soil is fabulously rich; my root system communicating and sharing resources through networks of fungus with other species of trees. Up above, my trunk and branches are exposed to the weather. There may be tremendous storms, and I may shiver and sway, but down below I have an unshakable core of calm. I use the tree metaphor in many of my guided meditations on the *Balanced Mind with Julie Potiker* podcast. I am grateful to the groundbreaking work of forest ecologist Professor Suzanne Simard, who stayed the course in her now validated, painstaking research, allowing my guided meditations in which the tree roots are communicating to be rooted (pun intended!) in science. She was the inspiration for one of the characters in the Pulitzer Prize winning novel, *Understory,* by Richard Powers. That book changed my life.

Let's examine how SNAP functions for equanimity in the following story:

FALLING OFF THE TIGHTROPE

The other day I was driving down the road thinking, *I just can't take this suffering for one more minute!* Then I answered myself with "Of course you can, and you will, because you always do—there is no exit ramp, no way out, no way off this roller coaster."

I imagined walking on a tightrope with little clumps of jagged broken glass on the rope. The shards of glass were transparent, and squinting didn't make them any easier to see; so each step was precarious, anxiety turning my legs to stone and causing the creases around my eyes to deepen.

I wondered what it would be like to fall, to allow myself to let go.

I did it, and landed safely in my seat, still buckled in, in the parking lot of Whole Foods in La Jolla, California.

Just then my phone rang, and I looked to see who was calling to decide whether to pick up. I generally don't reach out when I'm feeling like this ... but it was Stefani, my college roommate, whom I love and respect.

"Hi, I'm glad you called, but I need to tell you I won't be able to be any support to you on this call," I said.

"I'm calling to support you!" she replied.

Phew! That was the universe dropping a gift just when I needed it! We chatted for forty-five minutes, and she not only had a compassionate ear, but also some helpful action steps I could take to gather more support.

I was in the parking lot of the Whole Foods because grocery shopping at that store is a form of self-care for me. I was hoping that standing in the produce department would bring me joy, as it so often has when I'm feeling low. The produce didn't disappoint! Red, yellow, and orange peppers, leafy greens and deep purple eggplants, radishes and beets, all shimmering with fine mists of water—they were gorgeous, and it lifted my mood.

While considering the dizzying array of yogurts, my phone buzzed again. I smiled to see the name of a colleague from northern California and happily picked up the call. We chatted briefly but deeply, and with humor, because this guy always brings out the humor in me.

"Life is so crazy on a macro level in our country and the world, and on a micro level with me personally; but inside my heart, I'm OK," I said in amazement.

"That's your resilience," he replied.

That's it!

My resilience is my godsend.

My resilience is hard won from years of practicing with excellent evidence-based teachers from the areas of mindfulness, meditation, mindful self-compassion, neuropsychology, neurobiology, positive psychology—and I'm sure I'm missing some other "-ologies" out there—who have given me help and hope and healing.

Mindfully chopping the veggies in my kitchen was therapeutic, and the *gazunkta* pot of soup I created was balm for my soul. I made enough soup to have six cups to tuck into the freezer for the next time I need a warm embrace—a time I know is coming.

LET'S SNAP FOR EQUANIMITY

You can use SNAP like I did, while sitting in the car in the parking lot of Whole Foods.

Soothing touch: Place your hands where you find it most soothing—your heart, cradling you face, giving your upper arms a hug, hands on your belly, or hand in hand. I placed my hands on my heart, feeling the warmth and care for myself.

Name the emotion: I named the emotions, as there were more than one, trying to get down to the bottom, the softest emotion available.

Act: You could start with a breathing exercise, breathing in for a count of four, out for a count of six, doing this for three to five breath cycles. After that, your body will be in a calmer state for you to choose another mindful method tool. Here, talking with a dear friend was the appropriate tool, and I got lucky that she called me. When I got the second call while I was in the grocery store, it was gravy in the feel-good department!

Praise: You can ask the question "What should I do right now?" to yourself, and then do it! I actually drove to Whole Foods to make myself feel better because I was hurting. Knowing that being in the produce department lifts my spirits may sound weird, but whatever works, as long as it doesn't harm you or someone else, I recommend doing it!

One of the best mindful method tools I have found to help with maintaining equanimity is meditation. Meditation is foundational for SNAP. After a while, you realize that you are noticing your thoughts, feelings, and emotions without being the character in the story. It's like you are noticing anger arising, but you are not anger. It sounds esoteric until it happens naturally.

Stories make these concepts so much easier to grasp. In the episode below, I observe my train of thoughts blowing through like clouds on the big sky of my mind because of the equanimity that mindfulness practice supports.

THE SCREAMING CHILD

I had an interesting experience recently that showed me what a difference being a long-time meditator can make when we encounter spur-of-the-moment stressors. I was having acupuncture done for my sciatic pain— my "radiculitis" as I call it—when suddenly, I heard a bloodcurdling scream.

It came from a young child of maybe three or four, and the scream was followed by her shouting, "I don't want to deal with the neeeeeedles!"

My first thought was *Oh, you poor sweetheart! Of course, you don't want to deal with the needles!* But her protests continued loudly for the next fifteen or twenty minutes.

I observed as my thoughts shifted.

I watched what my mind was doing—just as we do in meditation, watching our thoughts and feelings. This interesting stream of consciousness went all the way from having compassion for this kid to having righteous indignation that my quiet-time spa treatment was being ruined; then back to thinking, *Who am I to have righteousness? This is another living soul suffering! Poor thing!* to beating myself up for my thoughts; then to trying to figure it out: *Why is there a kid in here? This is an adult place!*; then wondering, *Well, if they're going to treat kids in here, how might they do this differently so the main treatment rooms are separate from the pediatrics?*

At one point I even thought, *Wow, what vibrato! That kid will be an opera star!*

It was fascinating!

When the acupuncturist came in to check on me and ask how my session went, I shared my stream of consciousness with her.

I smiled when she followed up by sharing with me that she had been listening to the tantrum from a nearby room and thinking, *Thank God it's Potiker in there!*

She knew that I wouldn't throw a fit about the experience, like so many other clients might.

By observing my thoughts without judgment, I didn't get sucked into them.

And that made a huge difference for both me and the acupuncturist that day! Her response also gave me a chance to reflect on my own ability to observe rather than react.

That's the gift of practicing daily mindfulness meditation.

Soothing touch: You would apply your hands to where you find it soothing to calm down your nervous system. The acupuncture needles were taking care of the soothing touch for me.

Name the emotion: Name what comes up, even if the name changes as new feelings arise. That was my observation of the wave of thoughts, each one different, all in the same ocean.

Act: You might use breath work, or lean into the common humanity aspect like I did above, mentioning to myself this was another living soul that was afraid and deserved compassion. If you noticed you were getting angry, getting below the anger to your feeling of being afraid for the person opens your heart to compassion.

Praise: Give yourself a pat on the back for managing the situation with aplomb! When Ann Michelle, the acupuncturist, came back into the room and complimented me on my equanimity, it was a beautiful validation of all my good work!

And you never know … one day your equanimity practice might just save your life, or your neck!

KEEPING YOUR COOL IN A DANGER ZONE

Staying in the Saddle—Equanimity in Action!

You know that small voice that tells you to do something—you are afraid if you don't do what it suggests that you will regret it? At the last minute before I mounted the horse Checkers, I walked back into the tack room at the Miraval Life in Balance Spa in Tucson, Arizona and exchanged my cowboy hat for one of their helmets.

"Look at you with a helmet! You think you'll go down?" asked one of the other spa guests.

"I don't think so, but I don't want to ignore that voice in my head and then regret it later!" I replied.

So began a terrifying trail ride; one I am happy to have survived so I can share the incredible silver-lining story that unfolded.

My horse was in the third position. The first horse, Duchess, was being ridden by one guide, a seasoned rider and instructor. Behind her was a spa guest who was a beginner, only having ridden on a vacation once before. I was in the third position riding Checkers, followed by two fabulous sisters, speaking Farsi and English, who were both beginning riders, with one more guide bringing up the rear. I consider myself a beginner, even though I rode on trail rides with my family when my kids were younger. It had been fifteen years since I had been on a horse. Cut now to present tense, and come with me on this mini "movie."

The path is super narrow. There are rocks and cactus and bushes making walls on both sides of the trail. We are single file with no room to move. Suddenly, Duchess (the lead horse with the guide) rears and tries to back up. The guide is forcefully steering her straight ahead and spurring her to get her to comply. We all have to stop so we don't rear-end each other. When Duchess calms down, the guide explains that Duchess saw a deer up ahead on the ridge, and it scared her. At this point I'm thinking, *Great, I can't get out of this line, and the lead horse is not stable.*

I'm careful to make my body relaxed and heavy in the saddle. I note my breathing, feeling my body breathing in and out.

Three minutes later it happens again. This time Duchess takes longer to get under control. And then almost immediately Duchess goes wild! She is rearing up. She is backing up and stepping sideways. The guide is desperately trying to keep her from turning all the way around and charging into us. She is kicking the horse's flanks; all the while the horse is dancing sideways in reverse. At one point the horse second in line gets past Duchess and moves up out of the way. That leaves me, on Checkers, in the line of fire.

Everything goes into slow motion as I see her crazy horse eyes and enormous horse rear end skidding into me and Checkers. The whole time I am sitting still in my saddle, holding firm to the reins while repeating "staying calm, staying calm" over and over, loud enough for Checkers to hear me. Seeing Checkers remain calm works magic on Duchess. She eventually calms down enough so we can continue to walk forward, with the spa guest in position two now in the lead. Eventually, we come to a clearing where we can all fan out and regroup.

The guide says, "Wow, that was scary. Is everyone OK?" Everyone in the group comments on how well I handled the horse and the situation.

I say, "Thank you, but actually I'm not OK. I was freaking out inside."

She suggests I talk about it; she says it will help. So this comes out of my mouth: "When I was eight or nine years old at day camp, I was riding back into the corral with all the other campers. We were supposed to go two by two, with the first two riders splitting right and left inside the corral and taking the first spot on each side. Instead, the kids went straight, and all the horses followed them straight ahead, causing a jam-up of horses and kids. My horse got kicked, and reared up, throwing me to the ground. They carried me to the infirmary and put a blow-up splint on my leg that went from my ankle to my hip. My dad had to leave work to pick me up and take me to the hospital for X-rays. They thought I might have broken my hip. I didn't get back on a horse again for twenty-five years. When I saw Duchess's crazy eyes and her big back end swinging toward me, I thought, *F—k me, I can't believe this is happening again. Get low and solid. Glad I have a helmet on. Stay calm. Stay on.*"

The amazing thing about that memory and the feelings attached to it rushing out of my mouth is that I wasn't thinking about what I was about to say. More amazing still is that I haven't thought of the summer camp event in at least forty years, and if you asked me about it now, I would not have considered it traumatic.

Later that afternoon, I was in a floating meditation class at the spa. I was suspended in the air in a cocoon of fabric hanging from the ceiling. The teacher was leading us in a guided practice, periodically giving each cocoon a gentle swing while tapping the crystal bowels with a drumstick, making different bonging sounds. You could hear the birds chirping outside, the quiet music, and an occasional snore from a neighbor cocoon. Instead of blissing out right away, I was in a dialogue with my mind. Flashbacks of crazy-eyed, huge-assed Duchess were playing behind my eyelids. I was telling myself to snap out of it, that I would attend to that later, that it must have actually been traumatic, and to get back to my breath and this cocoon in this room right here, right now. My inner voice won the struggle, and I enjoyed a fabulous meditation floating in that beautiful room.

An hour later, though, I lay down for a nap and the flashbacks returned. I acknowledged them, thinking, *Oh, this is trauma. Sorry that happened to you today, sweetheart. You did an awesome job keeping yourself and your horse together. What should you hear right now?* Then I placed my hand on my heart, which I find soothing, and told myself I was safe and sound. I then changed the channel in my mind to replay the meditation in the hanging cocoon. It didn't work to put me to sleep, but it did interrupt the negative discursive loop of flashbacks.

Soothing touch: Place your hands where you find it soothing to start your feel-good hormones flowing. I put my hand on my heart.

Name the emotion: Whatever it is, name it to tame it. I named this emotion as trauma.

Act: You have a range of good options. You are safe right now. Just noticing that the danger has passed and that you are safe and sound is helpful. Ground yourself by dropping your attention to the soles of your feet. Take a leisurely walk, in nature, opening up your sense doors to what you can see, feel, hear, touch, and smell. I gave myself a kind talking to, and popped in a yummy memory to change the channel.

Praise: Ask yourself what you need to hear right now and tell it to yourself. Then ask yourself what you need to do right now and do it! I needed to report this event to the management.

The next day I sat down with Charlie, the assistant manager, to share the horseback riding event. I wanted him to know that I did not want a refund of the fee, rather I wanted him to hear what went on, and suggested that Duchess be taken out of trail-riding circulation. The assistant manager was a young man, twenty-six years old, but he had the poise and maturity of a much older person. He was apologetic—"You are not supposed to suffer a trauma at the spa!"—and immediately offered to see whether the trauma specialist had any time open for a private session, which would be paid for by the spa.

I had the most incredible experience with the trauma specialist, Brent Baum. He developed a modality called Holographic Memory Resolution (HMR). He took me back to the millisecond before the trauma, and we reframed the event using somatic psychology, color psychology, and energy psychology. We recorded the session on my cell phone, so I could refer to it later to understand what the heck went on while my body was feeling the heat of his hand on the back of my neck, and I was recalling long forgotten memories that had left little remnants of constrictions in various locations in my body. He assured me that my flashbacks would return no more, and he was correct! For more information on this relatively new healing modality, go to www.HealingDimensions. com. Full disclosure, there is not much in evidence-based research showing the efficacy of this modality yet. Baum wrote a book entitled *Surviving Trauma School Earth*, and has written articles you can find on his website.

Baum said the trauma that occurred on the trail ride at Miraval triggered the trauma I suffered being tossed off the horse at summer camp as a little girl. I changed the narrative in both memories while in a very relaxed bodily state, and surrounded each memory with a picture frame I visualized in a specific color that I then imagined breathing through my entire body. He suggested I continue to imagine breathing that color through my body a couple more times the following day.

Baum said my mindfulness and meditation practice allowed me to see the events on the horse as they unfolded in slow motion while monitoring my internal bodily sensations and being super present in the saddle on my horse. Thank God for my practice. I always tell my students this work is dose dependent. You need to practice daily, even if you think you don't need it, so it will be there when you need it the most.
My practice saved the day!

SNAP FOR GRIEF

G rief is a topic near and dear to my heart. It's a universal truth that grief is exhausting, harrowing, and can be grueling and unmanageable. I've experienced my share of grief, and have written often about how applying appropriate mindful method tools can help you hang on when the waves of grief wash over you and knock you off your feet. Grief can be close to the bone, from a loss in your immediate circle, or felt more broadly for global tragedies like the countless deaths and lasting illness from COVID-19. Grief can be felt for our planet's fragile climate, and can be felt for our struggling country.

ANTICIPATORY GRIEF FOR MY BELOVED FATHER'S PASSING

I was planning on sailing down the coast of California to Mexico on a ten-day boat rally with my husband and crew when my father's health took a turn for the worse. I elected to stay home, to be with my dad during what were his last few weeks. I wrote the story below during this time, as my husband, Lowell, was offshore sailing and was reaching out to me on WhatsApp through the satellite link.

KEEP CALM AND CARRY ON

"Honey are you keeping up your meditation practice?" my husband gently inquired. "This is such a stressful time. I really think you should try to exercise and do good meditations."

"Yeah, well, I'm using Insight Timer and doing a meditation for going to sleep every night," I replied.

"I don't think that's enough," he lovingly suggested.

I've been sleeping on the couch at my dad's apartment, hanging out with my sisters as we watch and wait for this beloved, elegant, and generous man to transition from this world. Today I realized that I was out of contact lenses. I drove home (a blessed ten minutes) to replenish my supply.

Once home, I wrestled with the choice to either burrow under my covers in my cozy bed or get my butt on the elliptical trainer machine (go down, ahh … go up, ugh …). Hearing my husband's whisper in my head from miles away out at sea, I stepped up on the elliptical trainer, put Donna Summer radio on my Pandora app, and let my feet follow the beat. I am so fricking out of shape; I stayed between level one and level three, working up a sweat for twenty minutes. Then I walked on the treadmill for ten minutes. After stretching and doing a little yoga, I chose a twenty-minute guided meditation from Insight Timer called "Coping with Grief's Difficult Emotions," led by Heather Stang.

This meditation is a terrific self-compassion practice. When I located a difficult emotion in my chest, she encouraged me to label it and examine the texture and quality of the feeling.

It reminded me of tonglen meditation, which I adore. Tonglen instructs you to breathe in the pain and suffering in thoughts and images, and use your power of imagination to breathe out light, clear, cool, peaceful air. It's like you are using your body to clean up the mess.

In my chest I noticed agitation and fatigue. I visualized a washing machine, the center post rotating back and forth, frothing the water around the laundry. The water was gray and heavy. I softened that area, much like a soften-soothe-allow meditation from my Mindful Self-Compassion (MSC) course. Then she suggested finding an area in the body that felt OK and focusing my attention there. That enabled me to switch my attention to my legs, arms, neck, and head. After that, she prompted me to flip my attention back and forth, from the neutral body parts to my chest. This technique is reminiscent of the "Loving Kindness Meditation for the Difficult Person," led by MSC cofounder Chris Germer, which was a lifeline for me throughout stressful parenting years. His many meditations can be found on his website: https://chrisgermer.com/meditations/.

At the conclusion of the meditation, I noticed the agitation was gone, and that the fatigue was now a lighter feeling of sleepiness. I showered and dressed in newfound calm, happy to be back in my true home.

Walking out of my bedroom, I came upon a four-inch piece of dog poop on my carpeting.

I had an instantaneous flash fire of anger at the five-pound culprit, still wearing her diaper while somehow finding a way to poop on my floor like a magician. I actually called her a bitch, which technically is not an insult—she is a female Yorkie! That cracked me up.

As I eased myself into my car, I took long deep breaths to calm my heart rate. My body was obviously overreacting to a little poop because I was raw from stress.

"Oh, Julie, sweetheart," I said to myself, "you are doing the best you can. Your best is pretty damn good. Keep calm and carry on."

Then my mind considered that slogan, and I got curious about who created that phrase, and all the merchandise using that phrase.

A quick Google search, once I got back to my dad's apartment, revealed that the slogan originated in war-torn England during WWII. It was designed by Churchill's war office, along with other posters, to help the public endure the dark days of bombing. Evidently the two million copies were never distributed! I discovered a charming short video describing its history and how the poster was discovered fifty years later in a dusty box at a little bookshop in England.

TOOLS FOR KEEPING CALM AND CARRYING ON

A great guided meditation for caregivers, recorded by me in 2017: https://podcasts.apple.com/us/podcast/caregiver-meditation/id1232945149?i=1000451285387

My favorite guided meditation to ease into sleep, by Kenneth Soares: https://insighttimer.com/kennethsoares/guided-meditations/deep-sleep-guided-meditation

"Coping with Grief's Difficult Emotions" by Heather Stang: https://insighttimer.com/heatherstang/guided-meditations/coping-with-griefs-difficult-emotions

Pema Chodrun's expert guidance on tonglen meditation: https://www.bing.com/videos/search?q=Pema+Chodrun+Tonglen&qpvt=Pema+Chodrun+Tonglen&view=detail&mid=E9DF550528ED174D7CF9E9DF550528ED174D7CF9&&FORM=VRDGAR&ru=%2Fvideos%2Fsearch%3Fq%3DPema%2BChodrun%2BTonglen%26qpvt%3DPema%2BChodrun%2BTonglen%26FORM%3DVDRE

Christopher Germer, author of *The Mindful Path to Self-Compassion: Freeing Yourself from Destructive Thoughts and Emotions* and co-creator of the Mindful Self-Compassion curriculum, leading a soften-soothe-allow meditation: https://chrisgermer.com/wp-content/uploads/2020/11/SoftenSootheAllow.mp3

My father, Paul Jacobowitz, passed away on November 15, 2019. When I understood his life was coming to a close, I knew my grief was coming in for a landing. As you saw in the story above, anticipatory grief is difficult to stave off; it's like you need a seawall to stop it from breaking through and taking you down. So, too, in the story below—one of my personal mindful methods is to take pen to paper.

EASING HEARTBREAK: MINDFUL METHODS FOR FINDING CALM AMIDST EMOTIONAL CHAOS

My heart is breaking. My dad's health is declining. He's so easy to love. He's such a wonderful human—so loving, smart, elegant, balanced, and supportive. I'm going to miss him terribly. But right now, he's still here, and so am I. Trying to stay right here, right now is part of my practice; it's tough yet rewarding, as we can still enjoy television programs and chatting about the past.

This morning I was practicing self-care by walking along the shore in La Jolla, California. My sister was hanging out with my dad so I could take a walk. I put in my earbuds and pushed play on unit two of David Treleaven's Trauma-Sensitive Mindfulness course. The course has five units, and I'm only on unit two. After letting myself off the hook, I had a surge of gratitude for the ability to take classes online, where the course is forever in your library, and you can pace yourself as your life allows.

During the session, David led a short meditation.

Following his instructions, I stood still on the sand and closed my eyes. I noticed that my body felt like dropping down to the earth like a stone. I absolutely could have collapsed right there, joining the sandpiper birds, searching for morsels at the surf's edge.

David then instructed us to open our eyes and notice what happened. I felt a subtle upsurge of energy, and my intellect labeled the emotion as happiness. Wow! I was happy to be on the beach, and happy to have found some energy to buoy the weight of my heavy body.

I'm not dealing with trauma, but I am stressed (who wouldn't be), and this technique worked so quickly and easily that I couldn't believe it! It is nuanced, as so much mind/body work is, plus I needed to have a quiet mind to notice what was arising.

How was I able to quiet my mind?

I can quiet my mind because of consistent mindfulness and meditation practice. With repetition, focusing my attention on the soles of my feet or my breath or a word or phrase becomes second nature. I've always said, "You have to practice with these tools when you don't need them, so you will have them when you do."

Today I gave myself a hug and a pat on the back for doing the work all these years so I could find my calm in the chaos.

Soothing touch: Place your hands where you find it soothing to help your body calm down. I placed my hands on my heart during the guided meditation.

Name the emotion: I named the emotion as anticipatory grief. You might be afraid when you feel anticipatory grief—fear about how the end will actually unfold; fear of your loved one in pain; fear about your role and whether you can manage. You might fear the aftermath. You might have anger it is happening. You might have regret or remorse. Whatever emotions you feel, please take the time to slow it down and name each one.

Act: I highly recommend getting out in nature. It can give you a sense that, although life on the planet is fleeting, nature is enduring. I also recommend listening to a guided meditation. I listened to a meditation from a course I was enrolled in. Being in a class furthers my core value of lifelong learning, which also makes me feel good. That is an interesting mindful method tool—if you have a core value you can support with action, it will make you feel good. For instance, if creativity is one of your core values and you make art, setting aside time to paint or throw clay pots during the stress of grief may help. If you enjoy journaling, or writing, setting aside time to do it can feel good. Poetry can be a godsend, if you like that sort of thing; I love it because it evokes feelings difficult to put into words.

Praise: Please be gentle with yourself. Go slow and savor any little gains in mood. Then lean into the truth that this is difficult and that you are doing it—you can do hard things. I used all of the above tools, plus I patted myself on the back for practicing for years so I had this foundation to support me.

LOVE FLOATS

Parents,
Brothers,
Sisters,
Friends,
Lovers,

Dreams,
Plans,
Hopes—

Poof!

Uncountable particles of stardust,
Swirling the universe.

Can we latch on for a bit?
Step onto the bottom rung to ride the "stairway
to heaven"?

Last dance, I always say, when I hear it … the
    final song played at dances in the Cleveland
    of my youth; a slow tune so kids could hold
    each other close.

Clip into the lifeline before you step so you stay
    tethered to the earth.

Close your eyes;

Feel the love stories riding the wind.

Let go.

Float.

GRIEF CAUSED BY YOUR SENSITIVITY TO GLOBAL EVENTS

Sometimes you feel off-balance but don't know why until you investigate your internal landscape and find grief lurking.

Recently I was driving home from an exhilarating walk on the beach in Del Mar, California. I met a girlfriend for masked-up human connection. Safely connecting with friends, getting out in nature, and moving our bodies are all recommended self-care strategies for managing stress during this most unprecedented time.

As I was approaching Will Rogers Beach—the Pacific Ocean was sparkling on my right, the cliffs of Torrey Pines State Park were straight ahead—I noticed emotions welling up in my torso and tears leaking out of my eyes. I let the tears drip and gently wondered why I was crying. Was it the exquisite majesty of nature juxtaposed with catastrophic suffering? Yes, yes it was! I didn't need to dig too deep to figure out the root of this grief.

The number of families grieving right now is hard to fathom. As of the time of this writing, we have lost over 860,000 American souls.

That's mindfulness in dealing with difficult emotions in action.

Soothing touch: One hand on your heart, the other hand on the steering wheel.

Name the emotion: Grief.

Act: Tap into common humanity. Tapping into the common humanity aspect of the suffering is important because it places your sorrow in a larger context. This fosters perspective and also helps you to feel less alone, which helps raise the bottom end of the pool—the deep end being depression, the shallow end merely the blues.

Change the channel. If you need a channel switch, do something that brings you joy and absorb the good feelings while you are doing it. For me, this last step was setting my Pandora radio in the car to the Carol King station, or what my husband affectionately calls "vagina radio."

Write in your gratitude journal. I made a mental note to write about the beach walk and view, as well as my luck to live here in a temperate climate, in my gratitude journal that night.

It wasn't until the next day, zooming with my dear friends from our mindful self-compassion group during our twice-monthly "Tea-Time" chat, that I connected the dots. Trish, a member of this precious group, shared that she has agreed to film and edit a video for one of her close friends, who is terminally ill, as a gift of her love and wisdom for her friend's kids. What a huge blessing that gift will be, and what an enormous responsibility for my friend Trish!

That's when it hit me. The responsibility of seeing what is real, of cultivating a practice that can hold it all with a clear mind and an open heart, is the practice; and it's not easy.

In the past two weeks, two women in the mindfulness and meditation class I have been teaching since the pandemic began became widows. One man passed away at age sixty, the other in his later years. One man in the class just received a lung transplant, and another woman's husband is in a nursing home in his sixties. There are people in the class grieving the death of parents, like I am, and the death of friends.

Praise: We join hearts each week to lift each other up; to fill ourselves with light to buoy our spirits. And it works.

Being in community helps to stave off isolation.

Isolation can lead to depression and substance abuse; both have a dampening effect on longevity. The Harvard Longevity Study, now in its eighty-second year, has illuminated the importance of relationships. "When the study began, nobody cared about empathy or attachment," said psychiatrist George Vaillant, who joined the team as a researcher in 1966 and led the study from 1972 until 2004. "But the key to healthy aging is relationships, relationships, relationships."

"Those who were clearly train wrecks when they were in their 20s or 25s turned out to be wonderful octogenarians," he said. "On the other hand, alcoholism and major depression could take people who started life as stars and leave them at the end of their lives as train wrecks."

The study's current director, Zen priest Professor Robert Waldinger, has extended the study to the wives and children of the original cohort of men. "We're trying to see how people

manage stress, whether their bodies are in a sort of chronic 'fight
or flight' mode," Waldinger said. "We want to find out how it is
that a difficult childhood reaches across decades to break down
the body in middle age and later."

Waldinger said he practices meditation and invests time and
energy in his relationships more than ever before because of the
results of the longevity study.

GLOBAL EVENTS TRIGGERING A PERSONAL GRIEF

Mindful Introspection: Identifying Our Self-Care Needs for Soothing Rattled Nerves

One Friday morning, I woke up feeling rattled. It wasn't
immediately clear why, so I used mindfulness to gently investigate
why I was feeling this way. I noticed that my physical body felt
tired, probably due to some leftover jet lag from recent travels.
Then I observed that it was Friday, which for Jewish people means
moving into Shabbat at sundown.

I don't celebrate Shabbat in a very religious way, but I acknowledge
it every week. It serves as a sort of separation for me from the rest
of the week's busyness. It gives me space and time to move inward.

So why was I so rattled moving into this Shabbat?

The Pittsburgh massacre in Squirrel Hill had just occurred the week before. My subconscious knew this and suffered with it before my conscious mind even knew the connection.

Squirrel Hill is the neighborhood where my parents grew up, and as a child in Cleveland, my family used to visit there regularly for holidays and family gatherings. Even if I didn't have this personal connection to the place, though, I would've still felt rattled.

The modern-day horrors of man's inhumanity to man—of antisemitism and the vicious, dangerous political discourse we have allowed—these things would disturb and disconcert me regardless. Since that rattled Friday, our country has seen more massacres, more senseless death and violence, including the shocking and tragic shooting of a friend, Lori Kay, at the Chabad of Poway, California.

Sometimes it feels like there's nothing new I can say that hasn't been said, no new wisdom to impart. In these moments—like that rattled Friday morning—I turn inward and ask: What can I do for me? What self-care do I need?

That day, I got my hair done; but truthfully, that isn't on my self-care list. It's not fun for me. It doesn't fill me up.

Spending time with my dad was a great comfort to me. I am lucky that he lived as long as he did, and that I had the benefit of living near enough to pop in and use our connection as a comfort, as one of the tools in my toolbox to help me feel better. The morning that I was rattled and realized it was likely because of the murders in the synagogues, my dad was still alive, so I went to visit him.

Then I did some writing.

Writing makes me feel grounded. After that I went out and spent some time in nature—another very grounding, healing activity.

Next time you feel disturbed or unsettled with all that you are navigating in your own personal life and as a human in this world, take some time and do something kind for yourself.

What can you do for you? What self-care do you need?

Soothing Touch: Place your hands where you find them soothing. This will release oxytocin and endorphins to help your nervous system calm down.

Name the emotion: I labeled my emotion as grief. Name it to tame it; feel it to heal it—as long as you have mindful method tools to manage the emotions, so you don't get swamped by them.

Act: Choose a tool that will help you right now. If you want to feel all the feelings for a while, and you can still get to the shallow end of the pool on your own and walk out, treading water in the deep end can be cleansing. Allowing tears to fall can leave you feeling lighter.

For me, that day my mindful method tool of choice was being with my dad, whom I love and who makes me feel safe and happy, and writing.

Praise: What can you do for you? What self-care do you need? Do it, because you are worth it.

I asked myself those questions and then followed through on doing it, because just like you, I am worth it.

EXISTENTIAL GRIEF TRIGGERED BY PERSONAL EVENTS

Sometimes grief is more dispersed, like an existential heavy blanket or dark cloud of sadness triggered by events in your past. In the story below, penned on my twin daughter's birthday, I use SNAP to move through this landscape.

FRAGILE, YET FIERCE: ALLOWING FOR TEARS AND HOPING LOVE WINS OVER HATE

On November 4, 1994, I hemorrhaged at UCSD hospital in San Diego after pushing out baby A and baby B. The doctors didn't notice uterine tissue on the placenta, which looked like a big mess of beef with two hoses attached to it—the two umbilical cords that were attached to those tiny humans for the thirty-five weeks and five days of their life inside my body.

During the eighteen weeks I was on bed rest, I reminded myself daily that my body was a better incubator than anything in the NICU. I taped a photo to the lamp on my nightstand that I cut out from *Twins Magazine* of two adorable toddler twin girls in a stroller. One looked like she was taking a bite out of her sister's juicy face. Both their heads were perfectly round, their cheeks rosy and eyes bright. I think their names might have been the Lannigan twins or Lancaster twins, and I sometimes wonder how they came out, meaning: How are they now as women? Are they both alive? Did they suffer much trauma? Did they have a "happy" childhood? Were they "typically developing" children? Are they highly functioning adults? Do they have a close relationship with each other? How did their mom survive their childhoods?

That night in the ER, the umbilical cord was tied off and disposed of; but a metaphoric cord continues to tether me to these girls. Of course, it does—I'm their mom. When I meet people who have no children, I am stunned by how much different their life is from my life.

Sometimes I feel sadness for them, if they wanted to have children but it didn't happen due to infertility or the fact they didn't have a partner during the years ripe for making a baby. But mostly I feel wistful, wondering how incredible it must be to have that much less worry, anxiety, and responsibility.

Then I tell myself that the price of love is worry, anxiety, and responsibility. That the price of love is grief. That the price of love is sitting with the knowledge of the impermanence of everything in the universe, and somehow getting out of bed in the morning and brushing your teeth, washing your face, letting the water in the shower wash away your tears, and starting again.

I miss my mom today. She loved those girls so fiercely.

She and my dad each had a baby to hold as they wheeled me back into surgery to stop the bleeding. I was scared. I looked her in the eyes and said, "I'm going to die now, aren't I?" She immediately responded with a forceful, "Absolutely not!" I can see and hear her saying it. She had an energy about her that was volcanic.

My husband, Lowell, came with me into the surgery, and was traumatized by what he saw them do inside my body to save my life. For days he kept trying to tell me, "Honey, I need to tell you what I saw ..."

I had bad dreams and waking flashbacks for months. I imagined a different scenario, one where everything went "as planned," where my doctor didn't need to be called out of bed to rush back to the hospital to save me, and where I wasn't beat up and exhausted and whiter than paper from so much blood loss.

I've gained some wisdom in my almost sixty years on this planet. Nothing goes "as planned." There is no such thing as "as planned."

"We plan, and God laughs," is the old, often quoted truth.

And speaking of God, I still don't know what that means, but I have occasionally felt a deep sense of connection to all things—to people present and past, to the earth, and to the cosmos—and although I can't put it into words well enough to explain it, I know it when it happens. And when I'm lucky enough to feel that exquisite event in my body, this body that housed three beings, I remind myself to be grateful for that moment, because it's not going to last.

It's fragile. We are fragile. I can't hang on to that magnificent feeling, it's too delicate, and I shouldn't strive to do so. Everything changes. The good thoughts, feelings, and emotions change; and the bad thoughts, feelings, and emotions change.

I feel so sad today. I will allow myself more tears.

I let some fall as I typed this post, and I will let more escape as I stand under the water in the shower. I will look at my joy list and pick an item or two to lift my spirits. I'll have lunch with my dad and his friends at his senior residence. These super agers are inspirational testaments to the human spirit—he is eighty-six and is on the young end in that community.

They have experienced loss of partners, children, parents, and friends. They experienced World War II and all the atrocities that followed. Some are losing their eyesight or are using rollators (the industry name for walkers, to make them seem sporty); but it is independent living, and they still have their minds intact. And what is beautiful and precious is that they are connected in community, which is the number one indicator for mental health and well-being leading to longevity.

So today I will sit with these wise elders and let myself fill up with gratitude for all our lives and for everything that we humans experience in our time on the planet. And I'll say a prayer for our country and our world. I'll wish for love to win out over hate. I'll wish for our country to unite behind common values of human decency.

Soothing touch: Place your hands on where you find it most soothing and supportive. The oxytocin and endorphins that cascade in your body will help you regulate your nervous system.

Name the emotion: Sit with the feelings and notice how you are not your feelings. I named this feeling grief.

Act: Take a look at your joy list and choose whatever seems best to support you right now.

My mindful method tools that worked were writing, choosing a joy list item and doing it, and going to visit my dad and his friends.

Praise: When feeling raw, please be gentle with yourself. Give yourself the time and space to feel your feelings. Change the channel with love, not to bypass the emotions, but, rather, because you are suffering and you want to take good care. On my daughter's birthday, I was gentle with myself.

GRIEF AT LOSING A PET

Grief for losing a pet is overwhelming. Even though we understand that the lifespan of most animals we keep as members of our family is shorter than that of humans, when they pass away, they leave us grieving. Here is how some planning with SNAP mindful methods helped me move through the loss with more grace.

TOOLING UP WITH MINDFUL METHODS FOR AN EMOTIONAL DAY

This was my second time euthanizing a beloved pet. Last time, when I took Dusty, our seventeen-year-old bulldog-shih tzu rescue dog to put him out of his misery, my reaction surprised me. I had to triage my body on the spot, throwing all my mindful methods at myself one at a time until I found one that worked.

This time, I was prepared!

First thing in the morning, I listened to a ten-minute guided meditation on the free Insight Timer app called "Relieving Anxiety and Feeling Grounded." Honestly, with over two-hundred thousand meditations to choose from, just figuring out what to listen to can give a person anxiety! Back in 2014, when I encouraged all my students to download the app, there were fifty-two meditations to choose from, and I thought that was a lot. At least they have grouped them by duration and theme, so navigating the app isn't too cumbersome.

After the meditation, I opened my eyes and listened to a podcast by Ram Dass from the Love Serve Remember app. While I was dressing and putting on my makeup, I was listening to His Grooviness teach a group of students about the universe. Sometimes I can access the part of myself that feels the oneness in all things, other times I think it's mumbo jumbo. I guess it depends on what I put in my mind, and where I want my mind to take me.

I put Ram Dass on pause and went to put Cosmo, our dear old cat who acted more like a dog in all the best ways, in his cat carrier. We drove down the street to the vet, and I signed the papers.

When they took Cosmo away to put in his IV port, I pushed play and listened to the rest of Ram Dass talking about the veil, energy, and the "other side." Cosmo died quickly and painlessly, with me stroking his fur and whispering in his ear that I would see him on the other side.

I can't remember ever using that term before, and it felt so right saying it at that moment because I believed it with all my heart.

My chest had the warm wide-open feeling I get during loving kindness meditation, where I feel like I am radiating love.

The rest of the day, I enjoyed spending time with my sister, who was in town visiting our dad. It was her birthday, and as she lives three thousand miles away, we don't get to hang out on our birthdays too often. We had lunch at the beach in La Jolla, looking out at the sparkling Pacific Ocean. Watching the waves rolling in and out was the perfect mindful method to add to the good choices I had made.

Checking another off my joy list, my sister and I luxuriated with our toes in warm sudsy water and our fingertips caressing glass beads in bowls of warm water. A manicure and pedicure are high on my hit parade of self-care, and I am grateful that I could make it happen. That activity did double duty, as I felt the gratitude with the joy, letting it land and rewire my brain for more happiness and resilience. It creates an upward spiral, an antidote to sadness and despair.

As the sun put the day to bed, I reflected on how well advanced planning works when you have mindful methods at the ready.

Soothing touch: Place your hand or hands on your body where you find it soothing. The natural release of feel-good hormones will help regulate your nervous system. I had my hand on my heart during the meditation.

Name the emotion: Slow down so you can put into words what you are feeling. Instead of a general grab bag, like "I am freaking out," see whether you can tease apart the freak out into its components, like anger, fear, sadness, or grief. Your thinking brain comes online while you are labeling the emotions, and that will help you calm down. I named the fear and sadness.

Act: If you know in advance you are euthanizing a pet, you can do the prep work in advance like I did here. After the veterinarian office, I hit my joy list with my sister, a double scoop of goodness.

Praise: Losing a pet is so painful. They are a source of unconditional love. They enhance our life in countless ways. Just being near them, gazing into their eyes, and stroking their fur drops our blood pressure and heart rate. After they are gone, there is a hole in the house and in our lives. The self-compassionate thing to do is to take care of yourself. I took care of myself all day with love.

I can't have a chapter on grief without including the most complicated grief I have suffered, that of losing my mom on February 29, 2016. This story was written twelve months after her passing. I used writing as one of my mindful methods in processing my grief. The first story I am not going to SNAP. I want it to sit as a foundation for the stories that follow.

REFLECTIONS ON 365 DAYS OF SORROW AND HEALING

My mom took her last breath at 3:10 p.m. on February 29, 2016. I whispered the Shema prayer in her ear and urged her to "go with God" before she became still. Although she and my dad had broken with the traditions of the Jewish religion years before she passed, as she neared the end of her days and the rabbi sat next to her bed, the religion of her childhood became comforting to her.

The past twelve months have been a journey I could not have anticipated nor understood from reading books on grief. In the mindfulness world, when I am teaching students how to feel emotions as sensations in their bodies and how to have a "knowingness" in their bones, we call this a "felt sense." There is no way I could have had a felt sense of losing my mother until I actually lost her.

The first couple of months, I was haunted by flashbacks of her final weeks and days. I felt enormous anger at the hospice we used, because of their enormous shortcomings, and I felt a deep sorrow I couldn't alleviate her fear of dying. I was also worried—and this sounds crazy—about whether she was OK wherever she went after she died. She was never comfortable alone. I am a logical person, so sharing I was worried about someone after they had departed this earth sounds bizarre. But that's the truth. I felt worried that she was scared.

As time went on, my bad memories were replaced by sweet memories. That's what the books on grief say might happen. Each holiday got a little easier than the last, but Thanksgiving, birthdays, and my parents' anniversary were tough. It was difficult to know whether to raise the issue with my dad. On what would have been my folk's sixty-fifth anniversary, my sisters and I decided not to mention it for fear of upsetting him. We were hanging out with him, not mentioning the white elephant in the room. We found out days later that he thought we forgot about their anniversary! My sister flew to San Diego from Miami just to hang out and not mention the anniversary. So now we say the words—today I asked my dad whether he wanted to light a candle for the anniversary of my mom's passing.

When February rolled along, I felt like my grief process was sliding backward. I was having visceral memories of last February. Images I thought I had let go were popping up, with emotions attached that were raw, just like at this time last year. I've done so much good work—so much

mindfulness, meditation, and self-compassion work—
so I was surprised this muck was bubbling back up in
me. Clinical psychologist Jackson Rainer explains that
a "sudden temporary upsurge of grief" (STUG) can be
so intense and unexpected that it can wipe you out. His
suggestions fit into my SNAP concept of managing the
difficult emotions of grief.

Where he says, "Identifying the experience for what it is
and calling it by name can help you stay in charge, even
when feeling out of control," this is the N in SNAP—
naming the emotion.

Where he recommends,

Remember that a STUG is a temporary, transitional
experience. No one ever dies from a STUG, though many
feel like the experience is deadly. The painful feelings
will pass. The most effective strategy in the presence of
a STUG is to ride it out. Find a safe place, as private as
possible, breathe deeply and lean into it. Allow the pain
until it passes. During a STUG, a person's body goes on
hyper-alert, releasing endorphins because of the fight-
flight response manifest in the perception of danger. After
the STUG passes, a body needs several hours to absorb
the hormones and brain chemicals and return to baseline.

That is the A in SNAP—act.

Where he offers,

Sleep on it. The day following a STUG, cognitive capacities return to normal, allowing more thoughtful consideration of the meaning of what triggered the memory. Take it as a matter of truth that the STUG signaled a reconsideration of a loving experience in the history of the relationship. ["The Blindside Wipeout of Grief," Jackson Rainer, June 1, 2020, nextavenue.org.]

This step works perfectly for the P in SNAP—praise.

Last week I had an incredible session with my therapist. I told her in graphic detail about the surgery and hospital visits during the last year of my mom's life. I told her about the last month of my mom's life and her last week at home, where she passed away. I told her what I saw and how I felt about what I saw. My therapist said, "Now you will feel better. You never told me all this before." It was as if she waved a magic wand. I walked out of her office feeling lighter than when I walked in.

For this past week, I have been reflecting on what occurred in therapy that resulted in my incredible lightness of being. Here is what I have discovered so far: No matter how much personal development I have done, and no matter how many friends I have that wish to be supportive, there is nothing as liberating as pouring my guts out to my therapist, because I don't have to worry about the effect my story has on her. I don't have to take care of her. She has a professional coat of armor.

I lighted a candle and said a prayer for my mom last night. Today begins anew.

These stories were penned when the loss of my mom was fresh and raw.

REMEMBERING MY MOTHER ON YOM KIPPUR

On the second day of Yom Kippur, I was teaching meditation at a synagogue to a group of hungry and tired middle-aged people. Hungry because it is a day of fasting; tired because they were hungry. It was my first time teaching at the temple, and I wasn't sure what to expect. I accepted the "job" (volunteering) because I thought this Yom Kippur, the first Yom Kippur since my mom passed away, maybe being in temple would feel good. Ten days earlier on Rosh Hashanah, we had a family dinner, and my mom's absence was palpable. I ended the night with such heaviness in my heart, with pain in my ears, and with tears in my eyes. So, going to temple had to be better than that.

When I shared with the students that my mom had recently passed away and that I had started the Balanced Mind Meditation Center at the Lawrence Family Jewish Community Center, Jacobs Family Campus (JCC) in La Jolla in her memory, the woman in the front row asked, "What was your mother's name?'"

"Ruth Jacobowitz," I replied. "Why?"

She got this dreamy look on her face and held out her arm. She said my mom was here in the room and that she was so proud of me. She felt goose bumps on her arm.

That was the third time that someone had told me they felt my mom's presence in the room with me. These people all have something in common, something about energy. I'm not saying I don't believe them. I want to believe them. It feels good and hopeful to believe them. And I know that just because I don't understand something, and can't prove something, doesn't mean it doesn't exist.

The first time it happened sort of freaked me out. I was having a massage, and the therapist—whom I know, trust, and love—had this whoosh up his arms and said that my mom said, "You are the one!" loudly and clearly. We didn't know how to interpret her message. I am the one to do what? To make a ceremony for her? To take care of my dad? To try to make a difference in the world? She had just passed away a few days before. He said she was still around, which freaked me out even more.

About six weeks after her passing, I visited an energy healer who shared with me that my mom was busy on the other side. She was annoying her handlers with questions about what was next, and she was trying to control her new environment. That sounded like the Ruth I knew!

The healer said that when my mom left her body, she was guided by her mom and another couple, a man and a woman. I imagine that might have been her grandparents. But who knows? As crazy as it sounds, I wanted to make sure my mom was OK. I had been taking care of her emotional needs for the past twelve years, and I was worried that if there was an afterlife, she might be alone or scared. She was not comfortable alone when she was alive. She and my dad were together sixty-seven years, and she always said she would have to die first because she could never live alone.

I asked the healer why my mom hadn't sent me a sign. She said, "Well, I don't really know how to say this, but your mom isn't thinking about you. She's trying to figure everything out."

Shortly after seeing the energy healer, my sister Jan gave me the book *Signs from the Afterlife* by Lyn Ragan. In the book, the author explains how to notice signs that your loved ones are sending you messages from beyond. One of the chapters talked about how bird feathers can be a message from a departed loved one. The day after I finished the book, I had an incredible experience finding six feathers in my driveway next to my car. I wrote a vague post about it on Facebook, not willing to come right out with the feather/gift-from-beyond concept for fear of sounding like a kook! A dozen friends commented that the feathers were gifts from my mom. I keep them on my vanity with other objects I like to look at every day. They are precious. I found one more feather a week later, and I keep it in my car. I also wear something of my mother's every day. I feel like I am keeping a warm connection to her when I can touch something that was hers.

I stayed at temple for seven hours that Yom Kippur. After my meditation class, I sat through four services in a row. The community in the sanctuary was the perfect container to experience all my longing and loss and heartbreak. I was fortunate to be sitting with two wonderful women for the memorial prayer service. Laurie had lost her brother, husband, and mother. She knows more about loss and grief than I do, times ten. She grabbed my hand and told me I had a fabulous mom. I said, "You did too," through tears that felt lighter than the tears I'd shed ten days earlier on Rosh Hashanah. My chest felt lighter too. Maybe I needed to be in a place where I could tap into the felt sense of common humanity that I teach about in my Mindful Methods for Life course. We all have sorrow. Intellectually, we understand that suffering is part of the human condition. Feeling it in your bones is different. That is what is meant by a "felt sense" of something. I had the felt sense we were all in this together, and that made the experience bittersweet.

May we have people to sit with when we have suffering. May we be safe. May we live our lives with ease.

If you find yourself in a weepy wave of grief and you want to try to use SNAP to help manage your nervous system, here is how I did it that day.

Soothing touch: Place your hand where it is helpful. If it seems like putting your hand on your body might be awkward, or make the situation worse, just put your hands inside each other.

My hand was on my heart so much that day.

Name the emotion: I imagine grief might be your label as it was for me.

Act: Looking at the list of tools in your mindful methods toolbox, choose several tools that will be helpful. Anything grounding—like a walking meditation, concentrating your attention on the soles of your feet, using you're here-and-now stone to break your discursive loop of thoughts—may help. Writing or journaling may help. Making a nice meal for yourself, or a cup of tea, and savoring the experience may feel nourishing. If you can see clearly enough to be of service, that can give you a huge boost of helping hormones.

On Yom Kippur, I anticipated that I might be in a tough spot emotionally, so I intentionally took the gig teaching at the temple, knowing it would make me feel good to do something loving for others.

Praise: Everything you can do to love yourself is what is necessary when grieving. Staying in community was the most loving thing I could do for myself that day, and it helped.

I have so many journal entries from my time surfing the waves of grief after my mom passed away. Below is how I lived my practice out loud in hopes of helping myself, and modeling the practice for my daughter Cara.

MINDFUL LESSONS FROM MY MOTHER

When I bottle up my tears, I feel tremendous pressure in my ears, neck, and head. It happened one night after my mom was gone about six months, while I was with one of my twenty-one-year-old twin daughters.

So, with tears running down my face, I said, "OK, this is grief. This is sorrow. This sucks. OK, I named it. OK, I'm breathing."

Then I put my hand on my heart and said out loud to benefit Cara, "What do I need to hear right now?"

Then I said, "I'm alright. I'm going to be all right. This is a process that takes time. My dad will be OK. These feelings will change because no feelings stay the same. This hurts."

Then I said, "1 will pick a positive mental state. What should I pick?"

Then I looked at Cara and said, "I'll pick you! Sitting in front of me, holding my hand, looking loving and kind and beautiful."

Then I breathed her in.

Then I wiped my face of tears and said, "OK, that is the practice!"

I was clearly suffering—the SNAP method that helped me regulate my nervous system is as follows:

Soothing touch: Place your hands where you find it soothing, to tap into your body's mammalian caregiver response and start the feel-good hormones of oxytocin and endorphins circulating in your body to calm your nervous system. Both hands on my heart worked for me.

Name the emotion: It might be anger, sadness, or grief. I named it sadness and grief.

Act: Breathe and then choose to pop into a positive mental state and let it land.

Praise: Did it! The whole cannoli were self-compassion practices. I had the extra benefit of modeling the practice so that Cara might be able to do it when she needs it, which made me feel like a good mom.

WHERE I AM FROM

I am from the Random House dictionary, on its own
  built-in desk in the library, near the gold colored
  flokati rug—a rug that could tell tales.

From Fig Newtons and Grandma Claire's oatmeal
  cookies, delivered in the oatmeal cylinder box covered
  in brown paper and sent through the mail.

I am from the flagstone and wood house with two big
  blue spruce trees in the front yard, two apple trees and
  two pear trees in the backyard.

I am from lilac bushes running the length of the hedge,
  and my mom's green thumb making magic in colors,
  textures, and scents—red, orange, yellow, pink, and
  purple—which I sometimes helped push into the rich
  dark soil.

I'm from matzo balls and brisket and be dressed in the
foyer at 5 p.m.

From the Jacobowitz's and the Scherr's.

I'm from whoever guesses the color of the door at the next
  motel gets a treat from the vending machine, and
  always keep your options open.

From C's are not acceptable in this house, and you won't be in trouble if you tell the truth.

I'm from the scholarship of the Chachem Zvi to the atheists and everything in between.

I'm from Cleveland, Ohio—Poland and Russia.

From chocolate ice cream and black licorice.

From my parents eloping at age eighteen, and being together for sixty-seven years until death did part them.

From my father supporting my mother in her career aspirations in the sixties, before men did those things— she, soaring in healthcare administration, authoring five books, and lecturing around the globe with him.

From dozens of photo albums in storage—but my mom's perfume bottle collection, cow collection, and owl collection gracing my shelves. My dad's cashmere sweaters and throw blankets keeping me warm and connected, and a pile of his shirts lovingly made into a quilt that my eyes and heart love.

I am a link in the chain—going backward through time and forwards forever.

5

SNAP FOR GRATITUDE

THIS IS A DAILY MINDFUL METHODS TOOLBOX PRACTICE

Has all the buzz in recent years about gratitude practice got you wondering how to jump on the joy train? The benefits of having a gratitude practice have been written about extensively. Current studies reveal fabulous health and overall wellness benefits, including lower blood pressure, stronger immune system, higher occurrences of positive emotions (i.e. joy, optimism, happiness), more compassion and generosity, and a lessening of feelings such as loneliness and isolation. [Note: "31 Benefits of Gratitude: The Ultimate Science-Backed Guide," happierhuman.com.] With pandemic isolation, as we shelter in place, anything that lessens feelings of loneliness is a good thing. And gratitude makes us feel more gratitude. With this many benefits, it's nuts not to try it! If you skip a few days, don't beat yourself up about it, just start again. I have weeks missing here and there in my many gratitude journals. I find if I keep the journal near my toothbrush, I'm likely to remember to do it. One simple way to get started with your very own gratitude practice is to keep a journal.

KEEP A GRATITUDE JOURNAL

Start a notebook or journal dedicated entirely to gratitude. Then, pick one (or both) of these to try:

- Write down four things you are grateful for each day.
- Answer two questions in your journal every night:
  o   What are you grateful for today?
  o   What did you enjoy today?

You can write one-word answers or whole paragraphs. The ideas don't need to be monumental. They could be as simple as gratitude for having a soft pillow. If possible, make yourself write longhand instead of typing on a device. I learned during a question-and-answer session by Daniel Levitin, author of *The Organized Mind*, that the physical act of writing has more benefits to your neural structure than typing on a keyboard.

Whether you write longhand or type, you will still get all the health and wellness benefits of keeping a journal dedicated to gratitude practice. Robert Emmons, a UC Davis professor of psychology and author of *Gratitude Works*, writes that once you've embraced gratitude, give it around three weeks before you expect changes, "long enough for a behavior to become a habit. ... Changes can be permanent," he says, "as the brain re-wires."

I use the two-question method, answering what I enjoyed today, and what I am grateful for today. I found the writing down four things method forced and annoying. It's a personal choice, so try it and see what feels more natural. I had a client who wrote in a journal each day so thought he didn't need to keep a separate gratitude journal. When I asked him what he wrote about, he shared that it was mostly writing about his frustrations and disappointments. I encouraged him to get another journal and begin a gratitude practice so that he would be wiring in positive thoughts, feelings, and emotions. When we let the story fill us up with the good feelings for a breath or two, we rewire our brain for happiness and resilience. That rewiring is what happens when we "Take in the Good," famously taught by Rick Hanson.

YOU'RE NEVER TOO OLD TO BE HAPPY: JOY IS AGELESS, FIND YOURS

You are never too old to rewire your brain for more happiness and resilience. There is a fabulous YouTube video seen by more than half a million people called "Confessions of a Jewish Mother: How My Son Ruined My Life." Selma Baraz, the late mother of James Baraz (of *Awakening Joy* fame) recounts how much she used to love to complain and worry, and how, when her son was visiting, he got so sick of all her negativity that he taught her a gratitude practice that caused her to eventually rewire her brain for more happiness.

The video is hysterical because she is already in her nineties, and her delivery and timing are just perfect. She really loved her life of kvetching, and I honestly think she was shocked that she could let that all go. But let it go she did; and her last few years were more serene!

How wonderful to figure that out, even late in life.

Start your gratitude journal today and check in with yourself in about three weeks' time. What positive differences do you notice? How are you feeling?

With something this simple and effective at your fingertips, there's no reason not to start improving life right here, today.

GRAVITY, COVID, DAY 4

I lace my fingers together into a carrier and slide the hammock under the bowling ball of my head sunk into the uppermost pillow.

Heavy, so leaden to lift,
Rocking the cables of my neck to-and-fro.

The cables are quiet now, thank God, no longer screaming hot—a moment of gratitude and relief at the absence of pain.

My torso pitched up, heavy in a soft valley of wrinkled cotton and flannel, drying as I cool down, nestled along the embankment of blankets beside me.

Heaviness in my eye sockets;
Heavy, the back of my head;
Heavy everywhere my body makes contact with the mattress.

My brain in my skull feels thick, a waterlogged sponge.

The thought of coffee a mirage in my inner landscape;
Coffee fueling the breaststroke up to consciousness;
My arms in my mind's eye reaching up around and down,

Up around and down,
Propelling me through the thick gray fog
Until I break through into the clearing.

Coffee to lift me into this day.

I sit up in bed, thankfully receiving a warm mug of coffee
from my masked husband.
In a dream state, I take my first sip and notice my face
stays relaxed—
No involuntary contraction in my eyes directly connected
to tape being ripped off the delicate tissues of my throat.
A moment of gratitude for the change, the gentle sway
away from pain.

I swallow a soft marble of goo connected to a ropy
rumbling cough in my chest.

Surrendering back into the pillows, I allow myself to rest.
As I gaze out the window, watching big flakes of snow
dancing a haphazard pattern through the trees, I am
comforted in my discomfort.
It's OK now, everything is alright, each day an
improvement;
Feeling another moment of gratitude that because of a
human being's brilliance in science, this virus is passing
through me, leaving a trail of antibodies along the path
to health.

MORNING COFFEE MIND FLOW 1/30/22

A dark gray navy ship is slowly gliding on the bay—three
little tug toys in a triangle in front, a bigger tug in back.

A cruise ship, tucked up at the dock, looks like one of the
high-rises got tired of being vertical and allowed itself to
gently topple, now horizontal on the water.

The sun is warm on my arms and chest.
My soft pj's are a swing-style tank on top,
Allowing my almost sixty-one-year-old body room to
hang out at will.
The flag on top of the next building is flaccid—that's
why it feels so hot.

My floppy hat is protecting my face;
If I stay on the balcony too much longer, I'll need
sunscreen.

Lowell comes out, asking if I felt the earthquake,
Epicenter Valley Center.
Our son's building was swaying in Little Italy;
Facebook friends posted feeling the shaking all over town,
hearing their dogs barking their heads off.

This place must be built well,
As I was contemplating my morning coffee mind flow,
I didn't feel the earth move;
Only heard the plane engines roar, people in cars bustling
about; if I listen really hard, birds chirping;

Only my awareness shifting from sense to sense.

I notice silk filaments glinting in the sunlight on the
green-iron balcony railing;
A spider's been industrious way up here.

Time to duck inside,
Sending out gratitude for the time to reflect,
For the solitude while taking in the busy city of San Diego,
Full of sunshine and warmth while the northeast of the
United States is bombarded by a winter storm.

Gratitude for the five senses that help my internal
landscape come home to my sixth sense, peaceful abiding.
A flash of interconnectedness—a glimpse of the elusive
last sense;
Peace on the inhale;
Peace on the exhale.

Gratitude practice is foundational to the SNAP method. It is a turbo-charged tool in the mindful methods toolbox to help improve your well-being. It's a little different than the tools in the A box—for act—that I use for in-the-moment mood shifting, because sometimes I'm in a neutral mood, or even a pleasant mood, when I write down what I enjoyed that day and what I am grateful for that day. Other times, I have had a horrendous day, and I need to reflect for a few minutes to discern what moments were joyful in a dumpster-fire kind of day. Some entries say, "Another day in the trash heap, but I did enjoy sitting in the sun with my morning coffee, and I'm grateful that I'm alive."

6

SNAP FOR INNER CRITIC WORK

BE NICE! BE ESPECIALLY NICE TO YOURSELF!

Being alive means navigating the waters of intermittent chaos. We can't control most of what goes on around us, but we can control how we respond to it.

That's where mindful self-compassion comes in.

Mindful self-compassion is all about treating yourself with love, kindness, and care—just as you would your dearest friend or loved one. When you're having a hard time, you fail, or you notice something you don't like about yourself, see how you can care for yourself in that moment rather than pushing through with self-criticism or ignoring your pain.

Instead of mercilessly judging and criticizing yourself for various inadequacies or shortcomings, self-compassion means you are kind and understanding when confronted with personal failings. After all, who ever said you were supposed to be perfect?

You may try to change in ways that allow you to be healthier and happier, but when done with self-compassion, you do this because you care about yourself, not because you believe you are worthless or unacceptable as you are.

Honor and accept your humanness. Things will not always go the way you want them to. You will encounter frustrations; losses will occur; you will make mistakes, bump up against your limitations, and fall short of your ideals. This is the human condition—a reality shared by all of us.

The more you open your heart to this reality instead of constantly fighting against it, the more you will be able to feel compassion for yourself and all your fellow humans in the experience of life.

Mindfulness is the first step in emotional healing.

Mindfulness enables us to turn toward and acknowledge our difficult thoughts and feelings (such as inadequacy, sadness, anger, or confusion) with a spirit of openness and curiosity. Self-compassion involves responding to these difficult thoughts and feelings with kindness, sympathy, and understanding so that we soothe and comfort ourselves when we're hurting.

Research has shown that self-compassion greatly enhances emotional well-being. It boosts happiness, reduces anxiety and depression, and can even help maintain healthy lifestyle habits, such as diet and exercise. There are over sixty research studies listed by Dr. Kristin Neff and colleagues on Dr. Neff's website, *www.self-compassion.org*. The publications are broken down by areas of study including, but not limited to, adolescents and children, aging, athletics, body image, caregiving, coping and resilience, parenting, gender, self-esteem, and trauma.

Being both mindful and compassionate leads to greater ease and well-being in our daily lives.

THE FALLACY OF THE SUPER WOMAN/SUPER MOM

As women, we are often expected to do *all the things*. And let's be honest, our families, coworkers, and others learn to expect this from us because we are so darn good at making it look like we really can do it all! The reality is, though, that with so many balls in the air, something is going to drop.

When something does inevitably drop, what's your reaction going to be? And perhaps even more importantly, how are you going to react on a daily basis to the juggling act you've got going on?

One saying I love to share with people as they consider their answer to this question is the old adage,

"Pain is inevitable, but suffering is optional."

How you react to everything that is happening in your life will determine whether you ultimately sink or swim. So, what will you choose?

LET'S SNAP THE INNER CRITIC

Soothing touch: Place your hand where you find it comforting when you feel your inner bitch rear her head.

Name the emotion: You might name it shame, or embarrassment. Sometimes it might be sadness or hopelessness. Just try to put it into words.

Act: Gift yourself with loving kindness.

When that negative self-talk starts up, try replacing it by mindfully saying things to yourself like, "I am beautiful. I am smart. I have value. I am healthy. I am strong."

We are superwomen just as we are, not because we can create an illusion of perfection for others. Be grateful for who you are, and be kind to your whole wondrous self.

Praise: Try calling yourself "sweetheart" or another term of endearment.

Have you ever called yourself "sweetheart"?

If not, I highly recommend it. It cracks me up every time, and cracking up makes me feel better. If sweetheart doesn't do it for you, come up with something hilariously, comfortingly perfect from your own imagination.

Lovey?

Sweetums?

Schnookie Bear? (*cringe*)

But seriously, if it brings a smile to your face and delivers sweetness with a touch of silly, you're moving in the right direction.

In life, the more tools we have at our disposal when things get tough, the better equipped we are to stop the thought spiral of negativity when we most need to. If something as simple as the word "sweetheart" can accomplish this, that's a big win.

So, find your perfectly sweet and silly word and use it to comfort yourself. It might soften things for you at just the right moment.

On days when things are bumpy, I can put my arms around myself and say, "Oh, Julie, sweetheart, that was really tough."

And you know what? It helps.

TECH AND ME

Intuitively I slow my breathing,
Feel my bottom in the chair,
Unplug cords in the many cord strip,
Unplug cords in my chest, arms, and hands;
Plug little blocks back in,
Shut down, restart,
Shut down,
Restart.
Is that the same as sleeping?

The monitor is a luminous black blank;
My laptop plugged in is a shade of navy blue,
reflecting my unwashed face in glasses; my
sleeping sweater bought by a dear friend that I
wear when I want to feel her hug … I wear it so
much it is fraying.

Light!
A monitor filled with little squares,
Illuminated Post-it Notes of productivity,
Chaos on the screen that somehow feels cozy;
Still unable to connect to Zoom,
Still unable to use my phone as a hotspot.

Tiptoeing into the bedroom;
It's cold in here.
My tech support man is in a cave of blankets and
pillows, the dog's paws drying on the rug after an
early walk down the snow filled driveway.

There are icicles dripping from the satellite dish;
Could that be the cause of lack of connectivity?
It's ten minutes until Zoom;
I've been patiently, quietly trying for thirty
minutes, or more ...
Do I wake him?

Oh ... if the network cable is plugged in, turn off
Wi-Fi on the tool bar at the top, he mutters, see
if you get Google.
No ... unplug, re-plug ... if it doesn't work, come
get me.

He's here now, in his sleepy head.
This is interesting, he says.
Got to restart it—I already did that.
Since we know the internet is working
And the Wi-Fi is working,
The problem is in your computer.
Do you understand that the problem is in your
computer itself?
Ummmm ...

He did it! My people! My tribe, there they are!
Twenty-five beautiful souls!
New faces along with old favorites.
I let go of the wish that I had on a bra, contacts,
makeup—be here now!

INNER CRITIC AND OUR APPEARANCE

My inner critic gets loud and obnoxious around the issues of my face, body weight, and lack of fitness level. It's incredible how nasty she is when I look in the mirror. This is a growth edge for me, I know I struggle with it and will likely have this internal dialogue forever.

20x magnification
Who is looking?
Is it real?

MAKING PEACE WITH OUR APPEARANCE: BEING MINDFUL OF SELF-TALK AROUND AGING

One of my core values is to allow myself to age gracefully without the knife or the fillers or any of that, but I've noticed myself coming into conflict with this recently. I notice myself smoothing my skin up or back in the mirror to see what I'd look like if I could just lift those wrinkles away.

I've also been seeing a lot of myself on video since I've been doing these cool, content-rich Zoom interviews with experts. I see the lines on my face and the skin under my chin, and my first thought is, "Oh! I've got to do something about that!" But you know what? I don't want to do something about it!

I want to make peace with my aging face.

I want to make peace with my aging body. I want to live in a space of gratitude that I am not sick.

I end up telling myself, "Hey, your face looks like sh—t, but you've got good content."

Wait a minute! Yeah, I've got good content, but *no*, I don't want to be telling myself my face looks like sh—t. I want to say, "Hey, you look pretty good for a sixty-one-year-old!"

I'm grappling with this. That's why I'm writing about it; and why I did a Car Talk vlog on this topic. I want to come right out with it, and I want to invite others who are feeling similarly to do the same. We're in this together!

When we reach for age-altering options, at some level what we're really saying is that we're not comfortable with who we are. We don't feel loved; really, it's that we don't love ourselves unconditionally.

We feel like we need to fix ourselves.

Can this unsettling emotional need to be "fixed" really be solved by altering our outsides, though? Doesn't it really just make us look and feel worse half the time (especially if you end up looking like Jessica Rabbit)?

My solution is to work on this "out loud"; to be honest and open about this all-too-common struggle in hopes that it can help others.

We owe it to ourselves to be mindful of our self-talk around aging and to give ourselves the gift of making peace with the aging process.

Lately I've been mesmerized by targeted ads on Facebook illustrating miraculous face creams. Truth be told, I fell for an infomercial and ordered some supplements that are supposed to help build collagen to give my face a more youthful appearance. I'll do research before I swallow any to make sure it can't hurt me, and if it doesn't help, at least it won't harm! You are welcome to join me as I SNAP this issue!

SNAP INNER CRITIC TALK ON APPEARANCE

Soothing touch: Place your hands where you find it soothing, as a reminder that it's hard to feel this way; you are giving yourself love, and the relief of oxytocin and endorphins being released will help calm your nervous system. I place both hands on my heart whenever the voice in my head says I am a haggard and baggy old woman.

Name the emotion: Sometimes this is a tangled mess, so see whether you can tease it apart. It might be embarrassment, shame, an icky feeling of vulnerability, or it could be a sadness. Name it to tame it—so it's out in the open and you can work with it. For me, I think it changes day to day.

Act: This could be a full-blown writing exercise like we explore below, or it could be positive self-talk, loving kindness phrases, and gratitude practice like we discussed above. Anything to make a shift so that you feel the truth that you are enough just as you are in this moment. I tell myself I'm such a good egg, really generous with my spirit, and that my compassion and love radiate from my genuine smile.

Praise: By being loving to yourself, as you would be to a dear friend, you are bathing yourself in compassion. You deserve it. And so do I.

INNER CRITIC MINDFUL METHOD WRITING TOOL

This exercise from the Mindful Self-Compassion curriculum is borrowed from the Internal Family Systems Model created by Richard C. Schwartz. I mention in my first book, *Life Falls Apart, But You Don't Have To*, that this exercise was a doozy for me.

We've all got those voices in our heads that speak to us in not the nicest of tones. Those voices are our inner critics. They try to keep us safe, but not in the best of ways. These are usually the internalized voices of our primary caregivers from early childhood.

NOTE: *If your primary caregiver abused or neglected you and this exercise feels too intense, you may want to skip it.*

If you're ready to take the wheel of your life and lay off that overworked critic (with severance and proper acknowledgment, of course), grab a writing utensil and a journal.

- Pick a behavior you would like to change. For example, "I want to exercise more" or "I want to eat healthier foods."
- Now write yourself a letter from the perspective of your inner critic. Let him or her really let you know how they feel about this behavior.
- Notice the tone, language, and overall feel of how the critic speaks to you. How does it make you feel? Does it actually inspire you to want to change, or does it simply make you cringe with guilt or shame?
- Next write yourself a letter about this issue from your innermost compassionate voice. Write to yourself like you're writing to a dear friend.
- Observe how different it is to receive input on this issue from a voice of compassion versus one of criticism. Which inspires you more? Which most moves you to make a healthy change?
- Write your inner critic's termination letter. Acknowledge all the years of hard work your critic has put in, and also acknowledge that this form of "pushing" doesn't work for you when it comes to making real change and embodying your healthiest, happiest self. Assure your inner critic that you can take it from here, and send her/him on her/his way.

What you think changes your brain. If you talk to yourself with gentleness and compassion and you take a couple of moments to savor the good feelings your compassionate voice brings up in you, that positive mental state rewires your brain. It is a simple practice with profound results.

Give it a try!

7

SNAP FOR PARENTING

As I began to write this book, the pandemic was in its eleventh month. Now we are in month twenty-five. Hopefully by the time you read it, we will all be back to a new normal, where we can safely send our kids to school without worrying about them contracting COVID-19. This pandemic has taught us all some unexpected lessons about ourselves, and here is one to take to heart: parents, your wellness matters.

During the pandemic, remote schooling and COVID-cautious in-person schooling has parents up to their eyeballs in simply making life functional for their kids. Internet connectivity issues, socialization concerns, and screen time worries are magnified by the reality that life needs to be lived this way—through the computer. Understandably, this has caused an upswing in behavioral issues in developing kids. If you have a child with special needs who normally receives support at school that is now unavailable, you have even more parenting responsibilities on your plate. Being a parent now requires an all-new level of skill and effort.

And most of the time, we do it gladly! Of course we want our kids to be happy. Of course we want them to thrive, and we want to protect them from undue strife or struggle any way we can.

But here's the thing: if we all lived by the saying "You're only as happy as your least happy child," we'd doom ourselves to a lifetime of limited joy.

Children are an immeasurable source of joy one minute, then a seemingly insurmountable stressor the next. Until we take our happiness into our own hands and unhook it from our kids, we won't experience our innately loving and peaceful core with any consistency.

And bonus, the happier and more at peace you are, the more able you are to show up with strength, courage, and commitment for those you love. Prioritizing your own wellness is a win-win for everyone.

Caring for yourself as you parent your children isn't easy. It takes planning, which can stress your already overburdened mind and body. I recommend using the SNAP system daily, and keeping a list from the toolbox handy so you can see what method will fit the time you have available to you.

Soothing touch: Place your hands on your soothing touch location—your heart, face, belly, arms, holding hand in hand—as a reminder you are giving yourself compassion, because parenting is hard. The release of oxytocin and endorphins will allow you to calm your nervous system. It's like you are parenting yourself!

Name the emotion: Oh, this could be frustration, sadness, fear, hopelessness, exhaustion; just think for a while and see what bubbles up. Once you name the emotion, your thinking brain will come online, and it will be easier to work with it.

Act: Take a look at the Mindful Methods Toolbox at the end of the book and pick a few tools that you think would work right now. I would use these four:

1. The Giving and Receiving Meditation: Breathing compassion in for myself and all the other parents who feel like I do, and breathing out ease and peace and light.
2. The Here-and-Now Stone: Choose a stone for yourself. I have a here-and-now stone that I wear on a cord around my neck. I also have one in my purse that my daughter Cara bought for me. It has a cool mother-energy symbol cut into it. I keep a stone on my desk, and one on my bathroom counter. I find myself reaching up for the stone on my necklace and rubbing it between my fingers on and off during the day. When you are focused on

your here-and-now stone—the color, temperature, and texture—you are in the present moment and not worrying about your child's past or future.

3. The Joy List: This method is a must! Make a joy list so that when you feel like crap, you don't have to imagine what might help. You can look at the list, pick an item, and do it! Remember with all items on your list to let the good feelings fill you up for a breath or two so that you install the positive mental state, rewiring your brain for more happiness and resilience. One of my best channel changers on my joy list is taking a bath with a lighted candle while playing music that makes me feel good using the Pandora app on my iPhone. Take time to investigate what brings you joy.

4. The Gratitude Journal: Answer these two questions each night: What did I enjoy today? (On bad days, it might take some thinking; but there might be something, some little sliver—looking out the window and seeing the sunshine or having a few moments of peace and quiet—that upon reflection was really good.) What am I grateful for today? (Even if the answer is that this day is blessedly over, that's good enough. Tomorrow begins anew.)

Praise: Give yourself a pat on the back that you are doing it! You might wish to be doing it with more grace, but tomorrow is another day. Love yourself up when you feel you had less than a stellar parenting moment. Forgive yourself and start again.

My specific parenting challenges led me to a doctor who recommended Mindfulness-based Stress Reduction (MBSR) to manage my extreme stress, which was causing speech disturbances—garbled words and altered utterances. I'm lucky my brain and mouth weren't working well, because otherwise I wouldn't have walked through the gate onto this path of profound healing. I didn't know the gate existed, nor that there was a path rich with decades of evidence-based practices combined with thousands of years of contemplative wisdom.

Parenting can be rewarding, but it is also relentless. When it isn't going well, SNAP for parenting is a lifesaver. In the story below, you can see how SNAP works on the spot for in-the-moment relief.

WHEN QUITTING ISN'T AN OPTION

What happens when you say to yourself, "I'm so f—g finished," and you know that, actually, you can't quit. Actually, you aren't finished … you are in it until the end. So what are you going to do to make it work?

Oh my Jesus, where does radical self-care start?

Baby steps! That's where it starts.

Yesterday when I was at the CVS to pick up a prescription for pain meds for my daughter, I had the wherewithal to buy an *O* magazine. I love Oprah. I've been following her since the eighties when she was in Chicago (I'm sure there are thousands of people like me that had the follow-up question on the tip of their tongue—and there, she asked it! OMG, she's brilliant!) Anyway, in my suffering yesterday, I knew that purchasing an *O* magazine along with my dye-free Tylenol and dye-free Motrin would bring me joy.

By the way, as a crazy aside, six months ago I had this vision of me and Oprah sitting on a sofa talking about how helpful my first book is to multitudes of humans. In this vision I was ten pounds thinner and had an amazingly tight jawline—nothing like my reality under my chin. So, my inner critic should shut up and sit down, but the truth is out!

Back to the story: I forgot the stool softener!

How could I? The stool softener is imperative to go with the Norco that the doctors gave her for severe abdominal pain. You cannot take a pain killer with codeine without a stool softener. The constipation alone could bring you back to the ER, and her endometriosis had taken us there enough!

I didn't realize I had forgotten the stool softener until later, after a cup of tea and *O* magazine had helped to screw my feet back into the ground. By this time we'd had some Thai food delivered and watched *Westworld*, and then I was like, "Oh no! I can't give you any more pain meds, honey, without a stool softener! The worst thing in the world would be to add constipation to your pelvic issues!"

Off I drove to Vons supermarket, the home of stool softeners late at night.

While I was at Vons, I was on my cell phone with a friend who really knows me and has walked through fire with one of her own kids. Luckily, she's in a good phase with this kid, but we both acknowledged how fragile that is, and how celebrating those victories is so essential. Anyhoo … I realized that I needed to hit my mindful methods joy list hard.

I bought a gorgeous bunch of roses. They were blush with a rose-colored hue halfway up the petals to the rim. I also bought a bunch of filler. And I bought another magazine—this time one from *Home and Garden* that is all recipes.

After administering the pain meds and stool softener to my daughter, I created a beautiful flower arrangement for the center of the kitchen table. Then I tried to settle down to sleep and realized that the self-care cup of tea that I drank around 7 p.m. while perusing my *O* magazine must have had caffeine. Ugh.

After a horrendous day in the ER with a kid who had considerable pain—but worse than that, had on sh--t-colored glasses—all I wanted was to drift off to sleep, out of this day and into another day. Hopefully a less horrible day.

Another mindful method tool came out of my proverbial toolbox as I put in my earbuds and pushed play on a guided meditation for sleep on the Insight Timer app. That did the trick; it overpowered the caffeine and allowed me to release the day.

I imagine parents the world over can relate to this type of grueling parenting day. Here is how you might SNAP a day like this:

Soothing touch: Place your hands where you feel supported: on your heart, cradling your face, on your belly, hugging your arms, or holding your hand in your other hand. Allow yourself to feel the care you are giving yourself in this moment. A release of oxytocin and endorphins will help calm your nervous system. Both my hands were on my heart. When I was driving, I had one hand on my heart, the other on the wheel.

Name the emotions: It's OK if you have a list here. See what the softest emotion is and work with it. Under anger, there might be fear or vulnerability. Take your time with this. The mere act of naming the emotion helps give you a little space around it, so that you can manage it and give yourself care, because it's hard to feel this way.

Act: Your favorite tools might be different than mine. In the episode above, I used some of the items on my joy list to give myself love. I really enjoy paging through magazines, and when *O* magazine was still in hard copy, it was one of my favorites. I also love reading recipes. Flowers give me tremendous joy, and I love creating centerpieces. Tea is on my joy list, but I screwed this one up by accidently consuming caffeine—call me human! And meditating with a guided sleep meditation works for me 90 percent of the time.

Praise: Yes, absolutely give yourself a hug. Parenting can be so hard, and you are doing it! You can do hard things.

MEDITATION INSTRUCTION FOR TOUGH PARENTING MOMENTS

- When you can, get in a comfortable position, sitting with your back relatively straight and relaxed.
- Close your eyes gently and take three deep, nourishing breaths.
- Find your breath where you notice it most easily. It may be the bottom of your nostrils, your chest, or your belly. Tune into your breath and watch it for a few minutes.
- Notice what's going on in your body. If you're in the middle of a tough parenting moment, those feelings might be frustration, anger, disappointment, shame, fear, worry, hopelessness, or depression. See if you can notice in your body where those emotions are manifesting themselves.
- Name the emotion and locate it in your body:

"Oh, that's anger in my stomach."
"Oh, that's shame under the anger."
"Oh, that's depression in my heart."

Naming the emotions as they come up helps provide a little breathing room around them.

- See if you can visualize what the anger, shame, depression, or other feeling looks like. Is it like a cinder block? Is it hot or cold? Is it shaky or still? Is it contracting, like pulling in and down? Is it expanding, pushing up and out?

- Then breathe into the pain. Focus your attention on your intake breath and breathe it right into the pain.

There is a space in between your intake breath and your out breath. Visualize that gap as a huge cavern filled with light. Your pain is dropping down into that space.

The pain coming in gets transformed by something in the cavern so that your out breath is a light, free breath of ease, goodwill, and freedom from suffering. Breathe into the pain; breathe out clear goodness.

- Keep practicing for fifteen minutes and then let the last five minutes be free from focusing your attention on your breath, words, or feelings. Just sit with your eyes closed and notice what comes up, allowing your experience to be just what it is.

PARENTING HAIKU STYLE

Woke up on the carousel in hell;
Is it a different theme park?
Pepto Bismol Chews taste like Beeman's gum
from my childhood.

SNAP FOR NEW PARENT FEARS

I had a phone conversation with a new dad who shared with me that his absolutely adorable baby girl is starting to crawl. He sent me a video; she is combat crawling—one elbow, the other elbow, and then dragging up the rear knee by knee. She's so cute! He lamented that now he has to make the house baby safe.

That took me back twenty-five years (my babies are now twenty-seven years old). I was a nervous wreck worrying about them getting injured! I told him that I made the upstairs part of our house into a play area. The stairs were gated at the top and at the bottom. We had plexiglass zip-tied to the balcony where there was an iron railing.

I had those blocks and little ramps that kids climb on and one of those pop-up tunnels for them to crawl through; little cardboard books for them to gum after I read to them and other teething plastic toys that are probably not recommended anymore because of some bad toxins or something!

We talked about the whole sleeping thing—how pediatricians decide the safest position to put your infant down to sleep in their crib. It used to be on their stomach, then it was changed to sleeping on their side (that was my era, with a little wedge in front of and behind the baby, who was wrapped like a little burrito), and now they recommend babies sleep on their back, with nothing in the crib—no stuffed animals, toys, extra blankets, or bumpers that could suffocate the baby if they roll into it. His baby has to wear a little helmet so she won't have a flat spot on the back of her head!

He was worried because he had put something around the outside of the crib—his baby had been sticking her little arm through the bars, as if she was sticking her arm out of baby jail. I laughed and told him to take it down; sticking her little arm out won't hurt her.

I said, "Can you imagine? We didn't even have seat belts, never mind car seats! Car seats that have to meet all these strict safety standards and be installed correctly."

He said, "Yep, I bet I came home from the hospital in my mother's arms. And there might even have been a cigarette hanging out of her mouth!"

So, the point is to do all these things that are recommended to protect the little bundle that you love more than anything imaginable, but to do it with a smile on your face instead of a pit in your stomach. It's the attitude that you bring to the task—the intention in your mind—that will make it either fun or stressful.

LET'S SNAP BABY SAFETY

Soothing touch: Place your hands where you find them soothing and supportive. Try different spots—placing your hands on your heart, your face, your belly, gently holding your arms, or holding one hand in the other hand. The release of feel-good hormones will calm your nervous system.

Name the emotion: It can feel scary having the responsibility for another human life, one that needs you for food and shelter. The idea that what you do has an impact on what sort of person you are bestowing upon the planet can be emotionally paralyzing! Just putting up baby gates and safety latches can tap into that deeper fear. Allow yourself to consider what you are feeling so that you can create some space around the emotions and work with them.

Act: Try this exercise:

Smile. Now, close your eyes and imagine your baby sleeping.

Focus your attention on the breath coming into your body and going out of your body, holding the image of the peaceful baby in your mind.

Take one more breath in and one more breath out with the baby in your mind. Now notice how you feel in your body. Notice any areas of tension and try to soften them.

Open your eyes. See how you feel. Smile to connect to your parasympathetic nervous system, and enjoy the rest of your chores with my wish that you have a little more ease to go with the grind of being a parent!

Praise: Remember that you are doing the best you can. Remember that human beings are resilient creatures. I learned when I was a new mom that a few bad parenting moments don't lead to lasting damage. Think about the fact that you are still here after all the not-quite-safe episodes in your history! Try not to sweat the small stuff, and keep leaning into love.

8

SNAP FOR POLITICAL
STRIFE AND DISASTER

When the COVID-19 shelter in place restrictions began, I accepted a post teaching meditation and mindfulness on Zoom for a congregation's learning platform. A few months into our time together (which, as of this writing, is twenty-five months later!) one student asked for help with her anger, which was eating her alive. She was having nightmares and was often boiling over in anger during the day. I got a few private messages on Zoom that the class wanted to be a politics-free zone, but here's the truth: our political situation in the USA is making people sick.

I teach tools to manage difficult emotions, so it's an appropriate use of class time—exploring what might help us all, whether our anger is from the fear that we are living under a would-be fascist dictator, or that we are moving toward a socialist-communist-anarchist government.

I suggested we need to *s-l-o-w the f—k down*. Slow down ... stop and slow down. I think the group was a little surprised I used the f-bomb!

We've all heard the phrases about hatred hurting us: drinking poison and expecting the other person to die; hatred corroding the vessel that contains it, and we are that vessel. Intellectually, I imagine hearing a collective "Duh!" But emotionally, it's much stickier.

How can we get those scratchy, jagged feelings out of our hearts and minds?

Telling someone to "let it go" isn't going to work. They need a toolkit to manage anger—some needle-nose pliers to pull out the jagged bits. Here is my toolkit, practiced over many years on anger and even sometimes on rage.

It starts with the three things I put on my website in 2014—intention, attention, and attitude. [https://mindfulmethodsforlife.com.]

Intention: We need to set the intention to let it go. Sometimes we hang onto anger because our righteous indignation gives us something that we need. However justified we might be in our anger, we need to let it go—which is not telling yourself that everything is all right or that the object of the hatred is suddenly a saint, but rather that the situation is what it is, and you're not carrying the weight of it anymore. I'm not allowing real estate in my heart to be taken up by toxic waste. If I want to be part of the change I want to see in the world, I need to lighten up my load so I can be an effective advocate for change.

Attention: I'm going to concentrate my attention on specific tools that will help me manage difficult emotions. When I notice anger coming up, I will pause. I might take a few moments to rest my attention on my breath. I can move my attention around, because the gift of meditation practice is that I know how to shift my awareness from thing to thing. I might notice how my body feels. I can put my attention on where my body is contacting anything in the environment. I might take a listen to sounds in the environment and note the temperature in the space and what colors my eyes see in the moment. All these objects of my attention take my attention away from the feelings of anger. This stops the ruminating anger that runs in a discursive loop, circling the drain with your body in tow!

Attitude: I intend to love myself, to treat myself as my dearest friend, and to allow myself to rest, as the poet Jane O'Shea describes, "in the hammock of my heart."

Then if I still feel activated, I will run through SNAP.

Soothing touch: Place your hands on your supportive touch place as a reminder that feeling this way is hard! Allow the release of oxytocin and endorphins to calm your nervous system.

Name the emotion: Labeling the emotion "anger" allows room around it, calming down the amygdala.

Act: I will allow the emotion to be there, to feel into it, not run and hide or numb it. I want to find it in my body. Put my hands on it. Then I might choose to release the anger and ground myself in the here and now by shifting my attention to all five senses one at a time. While I'm noticing what information is coming in, I can skillfully soften and relax any constriction in my body.

I intentionally change the channel, not to bypass the crap but to take back my power. I recommend creating a "joy list" for this practice, so when you are new to the idea, you don't have to remember what brings you joy. Eventually, it will be automatic. I know that a bath helps me, so if I'm somewhere with a bathtub, that's a "go to" for me. I might phone a friend. I might get outside in nature or move my body. You get the idea.

I must tell you that seeing photos of other people's grandkids makes me happy. I also love seeing other people's dog photos. I get the feeling of joy they must have—I can feel it expanding like a balloon in my chest. That's the feeling you are going for when you choose an activity that brings you joy—an embodied experience. If you enrich and absorb it, you will be doing double duty because you are wiring your brain for happiness and resilience. All those happy bridges are pruning out the negative and replacing it with the positive.

Praise: Ah ... what do I need to hear right now? I speak to myself. I say, "Julie, sweetheart, this anger is only hurting you. It's so tough to feel this way. And by the way, honey, you are not alone. Our country is being shredded to smithereens by hatred. Let's love ourselves up so much we can have love spilling over for others." I remember that, just like me, these people want to belong. Just like me, these people want to be safe and free from suffering. Just like me … Just like me.

So, let's all try to slow down and take good care of us. We deserve the best; let's give it to ourselves, then after we have calmed down, we can step up to help.

I had lots of opportunities to practice the SNAP method when managing emotions brought on by my use of Facebook. In the story below, I shared what was happening to me as I scrolled through my newsfeed.

RETURNING HOME

If any of you participate in social media, in the run up to the 2020 presidential election in the United States— during the pandemic and a long overdue social-justice reckoning—you would have witnessed a whole lot of craziness on Facebook and other social media sites.

I was grappling with how to communicate on social media with friends and acquaintances when they share posts that are inflammatory. Some posts are obviously designed to sow discord. They are premeditatedly conceived to get under the skin of a particular group so that, as anger or outrage arises, all critical reasoning stops.

That's brain science: we go into fight, flight, freeze; and our ability to respond rationally flies out the window.

Other times, posts are shared with elements of blatant lies that are verifiable. In these cases, I try to respectfully share articles from non-partisan fact-finding sites that tell the truth.

MY LIBERAL FRIENDS TELL ME NOT TO BOTHER.

In a liberal Facebook group I love, I copied a post from a pro-Trump acquaintance and asked for help refuting her points about how Trump was a champion of veteran's healthcare. It was interesting getting replies from the liberal group. They ranged from "don't bother, you can't fix stupid," to substantive content that was super helpful.

One member of the group is not only a veteran but works in the VA system, and they explained how difficult it is for the veterans that are able to use outside medical care to then get their bills paid by the VA. They end up disallowed, paying out of pocket, and hopelessly in debt. It's a tragedy. Also, only nine million of the twenty-one million veterans can take advantage of the policy, which was begun during the Obama administration and expanded during the Trump administration. I didn't know that information, and I am always grateful to be learning something new.

SO … WHY DO I BOTHER?

Why do I take the time to thoughtfully consider this stuff and do research to see where the truth may be found? Because we are all humans; we are supposed to belong to the same tribe. If we can muster the energy to slow down enough and hear what is important to the other person and let them know that they matter, maybe, just maybe, we can heal this great chasm. We all want to feel safe. We all want to be loved and to give love. Unless we are from a fringe radical group, we want peace.

Recently I took the time to reply to a friend who shared a post I thought was divisive. The minute I read it, I had that feeling in my stomach that something was wrong. That feeling is intuition that something manipulative and bad is happening not only to me, but to her as well. She shared the post because she feels so out of control with how out of control our world is right now. I get that, as I imagine we all feel stressed and overwhelmed with our situation! Our country is on fire inside and out in the middle of a pandemic! The post she shared was about "gaslighting," and it portrays conservatives being gaslighted by liberals. I find that interesting on two fronts.

The first is that psychologists called out Trump and his administration for gaslighting the American public for the four years he was in office. There are books and countless (I stopped counting at thirty) articles from a wide spectrum of publications accusing the former president of doing it and illustrating how he did it. When someone lies, and even gets caught on video and in their tweets, and then says it didn't happen, that's gaslighting—in other words, when they say that what you are seeing and what you are hearing isn't true, that is gaslighting.

The second is that if you calm down and pick the Facebook post apart point by point, you can see it is nonsense. But it reads so fluidly and sounds so smooth you get carried away, swept up in the waves of increasing anger or outrage as the refrain about being crazy gets repeated at each of the seven stanzas, causing you to fail to realize that no one is saying the things on the left that the post claims is happening! The author brilliantly touched on the hit parade of hot buttons in the long post, and then nurtured the reader near the end by letting them know that they are not crazy, that they must listen to what is in their heart. Ending with a Sophocles quote, "What people believe prevails over the truth," really is a tragedy!

I'll share a smidgen of the long slog just so you get the idea:

Me, to her on Facebook:

I just realized what this really is, and it's amazing. I took it apart paragraph by paragraph, which I imagine no one would take the time to do, and look what happens—I think the 2 sides are mostly in agreement and there actually is no gaslighting. I'm going to copy and paste it from my notes:

> We see mobs of people looting stores,
> smashing windows, setting cars on fire
> and burning down buildings, but we

are told that these demonstrations are
peaceful protests. And when we call this
destruction of our cities, riots, we are
called racists. So, we ask ourselves, am I
crazy? No, you're being gaslighted.

There has been horrible looting and rioting causing
destruction. That is not peaceful protest. That is criminal
activity. There have also been peaceful protests. Can you
show me who said the destruction is OK? Because I've
heard it be condemned by both sides for what it is—
criminal activity. So here again, we are in agreement, and
no one saying you are crazy, so that can't be gaslighting.
It's this author making you feel like "people" would say
that.

I'm going to lump these next two together:

But we are told capitalism is an oppressive
system designed to keep people down. So,
we ask ourselves, am I crazy? No, you're
being gaslighted.

But we are told that Communism is the
fairest, most equitable, freest and most
prosperous economic system in the world.
So, we ask ourselves, am I crazy? No,
you're being gaslighted.

This again is a difference in ideology, but one that no
one running for president is advocating. The Democrats
and the Republicans do not want communism. The

statement above is inflammatory to get conservatives to think that liberals think that—maybe some do, but not the people running on the democratic ticket. So where is the gaslighting? The author of this (probably in Russia) did a good job trying to make people upset.

Please people … saying liberals are drinking Kool-Aid and that conservatives are stupid and brainwashed is a cop out. That's an excuse to not do the work to try to understand how we ended up here, and it's not how we will get out of here without tearing each other to pieces.

I remember my mom asking me to show her my tongue when I was three years old after she'd found the baby aspirin bottle floating in the toilet. I was afraid to open my mouth—scared that I'd be in trouble for climbing to the top of the closet and eating all the "candy." She got down on her knees and looked into my eyes and said, "You will never get in trouble for telling the truth." So, I opened my mouth, showed my bright orange tongue, and got serum of Ipecac and a trip to the emergency room.

MY WISH IS THAT WE COULD ALL AGREE THAT LYING IS BAD AND THAT TELLING THE TRUTH IS GOOD.

That's a pretty low bar! We learned that by the time we were three years old! No one should get a free pass on the core value of honesty. If we can still imagine a return to honesty, civility, and integrity, I'm hoping that together we can make it happen. Our civilization depends on it.

At the end of the day, in the words of the late Ram Dass, I want to believe that "We are all just trying to walk each other home." [Dass, Ram and Bush, Marabai (2018) *Walking Each Other Home: Conversations on Loving and Dying*, Louisville,CO: Sounds True.]

May we *all* be safe, may we *all* be happy, may we *all* be as healthy as we can possibly be, and may we *all* find some ease in these chaotic times.

SNAP works well in this type of situation, where you are safe in your environment and your anger or outrage is something coming up in your body from your reaction to information on your screen.

LET'S SNAP OUT OF REACTIVITY!

Soothing touch: Notice the feeling (that's mindfulness that allows you to notice the icky feeling that someone is taking you for a ride) and place your hands on that spot. In the Facebook story, I had one hand on my heart, one hand on my belly.

Name the emotion: This was interesting, because it was a general feeling of unease and underneath there was anger—it's often the other way around, where the softer emotion is under the stronger emotion. I notice that, with anger, when you peel a layer of the onion away, or a few layers of the onion, you sometimes find fear underneath. This time there was a gunky feeling of yuck; and under, there was anger that humans are intentionally messing with our emotions with malice forethought!

Act: Research and writing were the mindful methods I used. They allowed me to stay grounded in reality, and they enabled me to stay true to my value of keeping a connected presence with this person, who I actually knew and liked; who was being bamboozled by a carefully crafted manipulation that swept her up as it went viral. It went viral—we are battling a virus, so many germs to consider!

Praise: I love and appreciate that I show up with respect for my community. It feels good to be "that person" who goes high when they go low. And it makes sense to do it when responding to someone you actually know, not a tangential "friend" on Facebook who you might never have met.

My business Facebook page, "Mindful Methods for Life," has a following of over eighty thousand people. I don't know most of them. I believe they come to my page for daily inspiration, hope, peace, and calm.

In June 2020 I shared a post on my Facebook page that caused quite a ruckus. I am mindful to not share my political views, as I want my page to be a place of calm for everyone. After ninety minutes of trying to moderate and mediate the discussion between those people who view wearing masks as a public service, those that see nefarious conspiracy theories behind mask legislation, and those that view mask wearing as dangerous to their health ("toxic tent," etc.), I deleted the post.

In the middle of all that craziness, a woman reached out to me through the private chat function of my Facebook page. She was vulnerable with me, which took incredible courage. She asked me whether I could recommend something for her, and we had an authentic, caring connection that can happen between two strangers with different views if we slow down our reactions and listen—really hear one another—and remember our shared humanity.

It was a bit humorous at first—she had told me to shut the f—k up, so I asked her if she wanted me to recommend anger management! Then I did recommend meditation, getting outside in nature, sleep, and being kind.

She explained that she was a burned-out healthcare worker, working thirteen-hour shifts, with scary medical issues of her own.

I encouraged her to stay in the Facebook group, to not throw the baby out with the bathwater, because there could be tips that might be helpful. I also shared that I curse frequently, so not to worry about the f-bomb! I ended our private Messenger conversation by wishing her healing, strength, and love.

The one line from the poem by Miller Williams that immediately rolled around in my mind after chatting with her was that we "do not know what wars are going on down there where the spirit meets the bone."

COMPASSION

Miller Williams

Have compassion for everyone you meet,
even if they don't want it. What seems conceit,
bad manners, or cynicism is always a sign
of things no ears have heard, no eyes have seen.
You do not know what wars are going on
down there where the spirit meets the bone.

The following day, I posted this apology:

> For a few hours last night, this page became a
> place of conflict. I intend this site to be a place
> for ALL OF US TO RELAX, and learn tools
> and skills that can help us live with more ease.
> I APOLOGIZE for posting something that was
> political. I learned from the spirited exchange that
> reasonable people can disagree on wearing masks.
> I see that specific scientific findings don't mean
> the same thing to all of us. We all have value,
> and are entitled to our opinions. We are enough.
> Thank you.

A different woman respectfully asked a question that propelled
me to do a little research. She asked whether the problem was the
conflicting scientific evidence with reference to mask wearing.
Her point was that people get their information from different
sources. The following is my response to her question:

> That's an interesting suggestion, so I did a search
> to find epidemiologists and doctors that say that
> it's just like every other deadly virus in which
> masks don't work and are unhealthy and couldn't
> find any current sources saying anything like that.
> I searched sources that I don't normally read, and
> found the message that masks are recommended
> to keep our germs to ourselves to protect others
> across various news platforms. Even Fox News,
> which was slow to come around to recommending
> masks seems fully on board. It's true that masks
> alone aren't the answer—people still need to stay

6 feet apart, wash their hands for 20 seconds,
don't touch their face (eyes, nose, mouth) are safer
outdoors than indoors, but I cannot find anything
credible from science to support not wearing a
mask, unless you are less than 2 years old, have a
breathing issue, or are exercising where your mask
gets wet, etc. Here's what I've found so far:
https://www.bbc.com/news/53108405
https://www.who.int/emergencies/diseases/
novel-coronavirus-2019/advice-for-public/myth-
busters
https://www.foxnews.com/health/scientist-
demonstrates-importance-of-coronavirus-face-
mask-use-in-unique-air-flow-video
https://www.foxnews.com/science/researchers-
urge-widespread-wearing-face-masks-slow-
coronavirus-pandemic
https://www.thedailybeast.com/hannity-lectures-
lake-of-the-ozarks-partiers-says-please-wear-a-
mask-for-grandma
https://www.cdc.gov/coronavirus/2019-ncov/
prevent-getting-sick/cloth-face-cover-guidance.html
https://www.tampabay.com/news/health/2020/
06/16/politifact-claim-that-n95-masks-cant-stop-
covid-19-particles-due-to-size-is-nonsense/

I don't know whether she read my response, or whether my
research opened or changed her mind. What I do know is that I
need to continue to try. There is a school of thought it's pointless
to argue with people who hold views that seem illogical to us.

News flash: our views seem illogical to them too!

I have a yearning, a deep longing, for we humans to come together in spacious awareness to make the world a better place. That yearning is hope. Things look bad because they are bad—the global planetary pandemic is horrific. Our leadership in the United States is toxic. The president is continuing to divide us with his ranting and raving—we are not the "United States," we are the "Divided States" of America.

What if, instead of shouting at each other, we took the time to see that everyone wants to be safe and healthy? Can we please stop politicizing science? Every time I think we can't sink any lower in our humanity, the person in charge, the man some of us put in the White House, and who some people still follow like a demonic cult leader, takes us lower.

I cannot stay silent while we rip each other to shreds. If exposing one of my core values leads people to leave the community I built with love, so be it. But I hope that we stay engaged and have respectful dialogue leading to understanding. We can be better than the trash talk coming out of the White House during the Trump presidency.

We can do better because we are better.

SNAP FOR DEALING WITH POLITICS ON A
MORE GLOBAL SOCIAL MEDIA SITE

Soothing touch: How this actually went down was that my husband saw me exhaling with my hand on my heart as I was witnessing these comments zipping back and forth on my page. I needed to slow it all down, stop the madness.

Name the emotion: I was genuinely surprised, actually shocked.

Act: Here I stayed in connected presence for the first part, then rolled into research and writing mode for the second act.

Praise: Think about your core values, and get in line with them. That's self-compassionate. For me, standing in my truth was self-compassionate. Being willing to lose some "fans" by staying true to myself makes me feel solid and strong. I like that feeling!

Postscript on the mask debate: The Delta variant is now running rampant across the globe. In America, those in the hospital and dying of COVID-19 are those that are unvaccinated. Those of us that are vaccinated can still get sick, but will most likely not be hospitalized, saving the strain on the medical system, and saving our lives! I have made the personal choice to mask up again when indoors and in crowded places. I'm not publicizing my choice this time, just going about my business, hoping to keep myself from catching a nasty flu.

Postscript on the postscript: Omicron has taken the world by storm. I'm on week three of symptoms as I type this today on January 24, 2022. I still am grateful to life that I got three jabs, so I can be vertical enough to sit at my desk and type!

A few last words on us and politics.

CALMING DOWN TO STEP UP

Experiencing the loss of our known way of being these past few months because of the planetary pandemic has been emotionally grueling. Losing life and livelihood on this grand scale seems unfathomable. And now, in the United States, we are at a crossroads.

If we want to be part of the solution, to rebuild a country we can be proud of—a country that stands for justice for all, where honesty is valued, and where integrity is manifested every day— we need to calm down and be effective advocates and allies in wiping out racism and police brutality. I don't mean calm down and give up; I mean calm down so we can come from a place of fierce compassion to join forces with the millions of our neighbors who have peaceful boots on the ground already, and who are doing the work to move our society forward. Calm down to step up!

On CBS 8 News in San Diego one morning, I suggested how to calm down to step up.

We are at an inflection point. This is our opportunity to take advantage of the momentum of the peaceful demonstrations to win justice long term. Incredible organizations have been in the trenches, making progress and raising awareness for many years.

Here are just a few:

Campaign Zero
Showing Up For Racial Justice
Color Of Change
MBK Alliance
The Obama Foundation

During the interview on CBS 8, I mentioned that meditation is helpful in calming your nervous system and reducing your blood pressure, heart rate, inflammation response, anxiety, and depression. It helps overall mental health and well-being. Now is a great time to begin a meditation practice or to deepen your existing practice.

Giving ourselves tasks and a direction for change will minimize the feelings of being overwhelmed, because we are acting. Demonstrations pressure the political system, and it's there where the change must take place. It's going to come from a patchwork of local mayors, police chiefs, district attorney offices, and city council meetings, and the pressure needs to be held steady here.

I look forward to seeing what unfolds; I know we need patience, because it's going to be a long journey.

May we be safe, all of us, really safe ... and free from suffering.

The news—the good, the bad, and the ugly—and how it makes us feel.

MINDFULNESS IN THE AGE OF THE 24-HOUR NEWS CYCLE

If you regularly feel overwhelmed, saddened, or just plain mad at the constant barrage of negative news, you are not alone. And I'm here to tell you, you don't just have to sit there and take the bombardment.

I get it. It can feel like if you look away for a moment, you'll miss some crucial piece of information that could be the key to unlocking all the political chaos that's been spilling out over the airwaves the past few years.

It is tempting to stay connected to the ever-evolving storylines.

However, how are your physical, mental, and emotional states faring when tethered to the news? Do you notice yourself feeling tense or angry, not just while the news is on, but throughout the day as you're thinking about it? If the news is compromising your sense of wellness and inner peace (as it is for many!), it may be time to look at a new way forward.

Don't worry. You don't have to give up knowing what's going on in the world. You may simply need a backup plan for how to find a balance between caring for yourself and staying informed.

Instead, give yourself permission to step away and use mindfulness to shift into a more comfortable state of being.

Switch It Up. How do you typically get your news? TV? Internet articles? Radio? Podcast? Social media streams? When you notice yourself getting stressed out by the news, one thing you can try is switching the form and frequency of your consumption. For example, if you watch news programs every evening, try skipping that for a week and only getting your news from the radio for an hour in the morning or an hour-long afternoon review of your most-liked online news publications. Then the next week, try another news source and time of day.

Breaking the pattern of news consumption that causes you stress by consciously choosing the "where and when" of your news cycle can be empowering.

To give yourself the biggest gift, try taking a technology holiday!

Power off your phone, leave your television and computer screens off, and give yourself the gift of some quiet, reflective time. You may want to write in a journal, take a walk in nature, or spend some quality time with people you love. However you spend this time, experience it fully without turning on your tech. Get grounded into the experience of being fully present in your body and your life.

Drop Down. Take some time alone and allow yourself to drop down into your current emotional state and see what's there, not judging it but simply observing it with curiosity. This is the heart of what mindfulness is all about. It takes practice, but pretty soon you can tune in to your body and notice what's happening inside you.

Self-Soothe. Evidence shows that putting your hand over your heart—or wherever you most find it soothing—taps into the body's mammalian caregiver response and releases oxytocin and opiates in your brain to counteract cortisol, the stress hormone. Try different spots out on yourself and see what works best for you.

Practice Loving Kindness on Yourself. Ask yourself what you really need to hear right now. Should you be told you are loved? Safe? Healthy? Strong? Whatever you most need to hear right now, create a loving kindness phrase and repeat it as a mantra to yourself. You can do this in seated meditation, but you can also do it on a walk, in the car, at the office, in line at the DMV, or anywhere else you need to. Try this out next time you feel stressed, and see how much it helps.

If a whole day unplugged seems daunting, how about a three-hour time block?

And as for not watching TV, if you are watching a heartwarming movie or funny TV series—stories that fill you up with joy, not stress—there's no need to unplug from that. That's where discernment comes in. I advocate unplugging from the TV if you are a news junky, but not if you feel like watching *When Harry Met Sally* again.

Take positive action. When the news brings you down, you can take specific action to lift your spirits. One of the best ways to do this is to volunteer for or donate to a cause you believe in. I have personally given money to Together Rising to provide emergency relief to children detained in atrocious conditions across this country and to fund long-term legal accountability to end this disaster.

I also donate to the Southern Poverty Law Center and to the Anti-Defamation League to combat hate. I give to a couple of strong guncontrol organizations as well, and chief among them are Everytown for Gun Safety and Fred Guttenberg's charity for gun safety in memory of his daughter, Jaime, who was one of the precious kids murdered in the Parkland High School shooting in Florida.

How can we exercise control over our state of mind? We do what we can to help where we can.

We can be kind to ourselves. We can be kind to one another.

SNAP FOR MANAGING THE NEWS

Soothing touch: It will help when you feel agitated.

Name the emotion: It may be anger, outrage, fear, sadness, hopelessness, etc. Whatever it is, putting it into words will help you calm down.

Act: This could be anything from a technology holiday to merely switching up your news sources, and managing the amount of time you allow the content to take up real estate in your mind. Then you might practice loving kindness for yourself and others, and see how that feels in your body. Once you are settled enough to make a skillful response, you can take a look at what might be helpful and then do it! Taking positive action feels good, and it makes a difference for humanity.

Praise: Pat yourself on the back for the good work of regulating your nervous system!

DEALING WITH DISASTER: USING MINDFUL
PRACTICES IN DIFFICULT TIMES

It seems as if the world is ending. Just when one disaster blows through, another one blasts down with fury and devastation. The earth has been pummeled by catastrophic weather events—hurricanes, floods, mudslides, and fires. We humans were trying to manage the news of unbearable suffering on a grand scale when the unthinkable happened: a mass shooting.

Just when I thought it couldn't possibly get any worse, Santa Rosa, Sonoma, Napa, and their neighboring communities in northern California started burning. Entire neighborhoods were being incinerated, with fireproof safes, protecting passports and insurance documents, reduced to ashes. I read in the paper this morning that a one-hundred-year-old man and his ninety-seven-year-old wife were caught in their burning house as the roof came down. Then my husband gently took the newspaper away from me, leaving only the arts section. All of this suffering is on a macro level.

Here are the tools in the A category of Act to try to manage the macro stuff:

1. **Up your meditation practice.** Try ten minutes twice a day. Or twenty minutes twice a day if you can make time. Look for guided meditations on Insight Timer or the free *Balanced Mind with Julie Potiker* podcast on iTunes. Mix it up so that your mind is relaxing into the voice.

2. **Look at your joy list.** Make time to do one or two activities on that list every day. If you have been putting off making that list, do it now. Just free associate for a few minutes with a pen and paper and watch the list grow. Remember that little things, like a warm cup of tea or a bath, work if they bring you joy.

3. **Get a good night's rest.** Pay attention to your sleep routine and see whether you can do the things most professionals teach to ensure you are getting seven hours of sleep a night—no screens for an hour before bed, etc.

4. **Make time to exercise.** You will benefit from the release of endorphins. Exercise has been shown to be as effective as antidepressant medicines for people suffering from mild

to moderate depression. In addition to the endorphins, you can feel a sense of strength and power from exercise, which may help to counteract feeling powerless during this time of stress.

5. **Eat well.** Eat healthy food, slowly and mindfully. Watch your sugar intake, limit your stress eating and alcohol drinking, etc. You know what to do!

6. **Stay connected with other humans.** We are wired to connect, and it feels supportive when we share our burdens with each other. I attended a rally against hate after the horrendous political events in Charlottesville, Virginia. Intellectually, I knew that me being there would not make one bit of difference. Emotionally, it was just what I needed—to feel connected to five hundred other human beings who shared my values.

7. **Take self-compassion breaks throughout the day.** Place your hand on your heart or where you find it most soothing. Acknowledge what's going on—for instance, saying to yourself, "This is a moment of suffering, this is hard." Then connect yourself to the multitudes of humanity that are also suffering, knowing in your bones that you are not alone in your existential angst. Then tell yourself something helpful.

My mom used to say, "This too shall pass." I tend to say, "You are going to be OK" or something along those lines. The last step that I like to add (thanks to Rick Hanson's "Taking in the Good") is to try to install a positive mental state by using a memory, or the memory of a photo, that makes you feel happy. I often call up the image of an 11 x 14 framed photo I have hanging on my bathroom wall. The image is of my three kids when they were very young. It's adorable, and seeing it usually brings a smile to my face.

8. **Ground yourself through the soles of your feet.** No kidding, put your feet on the ground and send your attention down to the soles of your feet. How do they feel? Are you in socks and shoes? Barefoot? Cold or warm? Moist or dry? The act of doing this breaks the discursive loop of thoughts and emotions.

9. **Ground yourself with a pebble.** I use my here-and-now stone. It's the same concept as the soles of the feet. Feel it, look at it, notice everything about it, and you will break the discursive loop of thoughts and emotions.

10. **Get outside.** There are huge health benefits to being in nature. While you are there, see if you can feel the temperature of the air, the breeze where it touches your skin. Notice any smells, and really look at the sights— leaves, flowers, etc. If you are walking, pay attention to how your feet feel hitting the ground, how your legs feel working, how your arms feel swinging at your sides. While you are noticing all these sensations, you are not ruminating and worrying.

11. **Contribute what you can to charities doing relief work.** Giving makes us feel good in a couple of ways. Of course, it feels good knowing that we are doing our small part to help, and that all of us giving together can mobilize great assistance where it is needed. It makes us feel some sense of control that we are taking action in a positive way. Giving also gives us a dopamine bump in our brains, and the dopamine makes us feel good.

12. **Don't bathe in the bad news.** Try to stay away from television news or video news. You can read the news so you have an idea of what's going on, but stay away from graphic visuals.

13. **Take time to laugh.** Watch comedy (but not political satire if it gets you activated). *Curb Your Enthusiasm*'s last season is hysterical if you like the Larry David kind of humor. There is a new Seinfeld special. And any funny old movies from the Marx Brothers and Mel Brooks are good bets for getting you laughing. We recently watched *The Wrong Missy* with David Spade and laughed out loud all throughout the movie. Laughter really is good medicine!

WHAT IF YOU'RE SUFFERING ON A MICRO LEVEL IN ADDITION TO THE MACRO LEVEL?

Every day that I practice using SNAP with my hands on my heart, I tell myself that this is tough. I know that I am not alone. Right now, all over the world, people are dealing with difficult situations on a micro level while already battered by macro suffering. I feel a visceral connection to humanity. I call up an image of sailing on the ocean with the sun on my face and the wind in the sails; that simple exercise helps for a while. Then my anxiety pops back up. So what's a person to do?

The answer is to double down on the thirteen items in the list above.

Yesterday I wanted to take a nap. I was too wound up to sleep, so to help me relax, I listened to a nine-minute guided meditation on Insight Timer by Jack Kornfeld entitled "How to Transform Any Hard Situation." After the meditation, I felt a little better, but not relaxed enough to drift to sleep. I then listened to Christopher Germer's twenty-one-minute "Breathing Compassion In and Out." After that, I drifted into a peaceful slumber.

Hearing Chris's voice makes me feel better because his was the voice on the recordings when I took the eight-week Mindful Self-Compassion course in 2011 that transformed my life. I continued listening to his voice for years, and then had the opportunity in 2014 to have him and Kristin Neff train me and fifty-one other lucky people to teach Mindful Self-Compassion. I used my noggin and actively chose Chris's guided meditation. I'll make sure I remember to do that every day that I'm frazzled.

I'm clicking off the big thirteen, and will make myself remember to practice every day. If I feel overwhelmed with anxiety or sorrow, I hope one of my tribe will remind me to practice what I teach!

DEEP IN THE STILLNESS

Reboot, re-new,
Refresh, re-imagine,
Re-do, re-
Do. Do. Do. Do.

Heal yourself;
Heal your life.
Heal.
Heal.

Live your best life;
Live your dream.
Live.
Live.

Listen to these twenty experts;
Listen to these forty experts.

Listen.
Listen ...

What is calling when you release the neon shouts
to re-do yourself?

In the stillness,

Can you feel the metronome of your one precious heart?

In the stillness,

Are you holding the pain of an eleven-hour hostage situation at a house of worship—relief that the hostages were released, anguish that Hate + Guns = Terror?

Still holding despair at the last shooting in a mall, club, school, church, temple, theater, house?

After events smack us across the face and cosmic sharp talons grip our fragile shoulders with a brain rattling shake,

Hopes and prayers do not resurrect the dead.

No way to abolish the NRA, impossible to re-write the Second Amendment, an anachronistic document those hold dearer than the lives of their children and neighbors.

In the stillness,

No more cheeks to turn, the body throbs.

A survival suit gets spun, wrapping the skin in a
    layer of something strong—tough and thick,
    like neoprene for cold-water diving,

Go on with your do, do, do, do;
Re-do, re-fresh, re-new, re-life.

Wait,
Listen,

Deep in the stillness,

Under the wetsuit of armor,
Your heart is whispering ... can you hear it?

SNAP FOR DEALING WITH DISASTER

Soothing touch: Place your hand lovingly on your body where you find it supportive. You might try a closed fist on your chest with a hand underneath supporting it; or both palms on your chest, with the fingers of the hand on top folding over the hand on the bottom. Any way that feels good, place your good hands on your worthy body.

Name the emotion: Naming it will give you some space and time to get your prefrontal cortex online so you can make a skillful response.

Act: Choose from the lucky thirteen list above!

Praise: Give yourself a hug and a kiss for doing all you can to not only be with what is arising, but to work with your emotions to regain your sense of balance.

SNAP FOR SADNESS, DEPRESSION, SHAME, AND GUILT

MINDFULNESS FOR CAREGIVERS

As discussed in the chapter dealing with grief, I could support both my parents as a caregiver during their time of transition.

Whether you're a professional caregiver or an "accidental" one who is stepping in to support a loved one, it's really hard work. Compassion fatigue is real, and you can feel burned-out if you don't take specific steps to take care of yourself. I'm grateful that mindfulness helped me stay grounded and present while minimizing being overwhelmed.

Here are some mindfulness tips (and some lessons learned) that you may find helpful if you are in the role of caregiver. You may also want to share them with someone you know who is navigating this challenging role.

There's nothing "standard" about end-of-life caregiving. Every experience is unique, as is every life. It is likely there will be moments where you'll find yourself needing to support others in unexpected (and sometimes uncomfortable) ways.

You may be in a caregiving role to a family member or loved one not at the end of their life, where their situation requires daily care that could go on for years. This open-ended caregiving may give rise to feelings of anger and resentment at the person who is ill, which can spiral down to guilt and shame. It feels bad to be angry at a loved one who is sick, yet it's normal to want to have some peace and ease for yourself. When you are burned-out, your internal resources may be difficult to find, and when you find them, they may seem less robust. This is the time to tool up—to get your internal resources on board and all possible external resources, in terms of human resources, on board. Getting support from your community may help—synagogue, church, mosque, sangha—any place that feels like home, where you can be supported with breaks, meals, shifts, etc.

SNAP FOR CAREGIVERS

Soothing touch: Hand on where you find it soothing! This can be an intensely trying time emotionally, energetically, spiritually, and even physically, especially if you are supporting someone around the clock and not getting much sleep.

Name the emotion: This step further calms your system. It makes room around the emotions, and you are able to realize that the feeling doesn't define you. Feelings come and go.

Act: Use a calming mantra. To minimize being overwhelmed, stay grounded and in touch with your body. Try focusing on the soles of your feet. Feel your body breathing. Notice what you're hearing. These are all ways to ground yourself in the moment.

When my dad was near passing, I held his hand and repeated a mantra, matching my breath to his: "We're here, letting go. We're here, letting go." I don't know if he could hear me, but it seemed to calm to him, and it certainly was calming to me. It also seemed calming to my sister and my husband. When you create peacefulness for yourself in a challenging moment, you also hold space for others to tap into it.

Pause to give yourself an energy refill. Self-care is so important for caregivers. Commit to giving yourself time to refill your own energy coffers. Take a walk. Get outside. Talk to a dear friend. Watch a funny movie. Do whatever makes you feel good and replenishes you so you can show up the way you want to when you step back into being a caregiver.

The bigger and more varied your mindfulness and/or general self-care toolbox, the better. This isn't a time to rely on a single method; you need options so you can help yourself feel better whether you're there holding a loved one's hand, on the go from point A to point B, or actually taking a few moments to yourself. For example, you might not have patience for a guided meditation in a given moment, but you might have patience to take a walk.

You might not have patience to sit and read a spirituality book, but you might have patience to watch a funny movie. Stay open. Allow yourself to use the right tool for the moment.

Praise: Be gentle with yourself. Being a caregiver isn't easy. Slow down. Listen to yourself. Listen to your loved one. Do what you can, and accept what you can do—and what you can't—without judgment or expectation.

If you are a professional caregiver, there are tips to help deal with burnout on the job. I teach the Mindful Self-Compassion adaptation for healthcare workers. All the usual self-care advice is important, but those tips require you to be off duty. While you are on duty, try stopping and taking three conscious breaths; breathing in for yourself and out for the patient; grounding through the soles of your feet; leaving footprints in your mind as you release one patient and encounter another; using the hand sanitizer as you enter each room and taking a few seconds to feel your hands rubbing together.

OPENING AND CLOSING YOUR HEART: MINDFUL EMOTIONAL PROTECTION

This falls under the Act in SNAP; you can do it quickly when you feel yourself edging toward the window ledge in what Dan Siegel and David Treleaven call "the window of tolerance." [Treleaven, David (2018) *Trauma-Sensitive Mindfulness*, New York: W.W. Norton Company.]

Have you ever heard about opening your heart? Or closing your heart when your open heart feels too much emotion? Mindfulness teachers and mindful self-compassion teachers talk in these terms, but it's a little vague and abstract until you notice an upwelling of some rush of feeling and want to tame it, cool it down, or calm it down.

A perfect example of this practice happened recently.

One morning as I was scrolling through my Facebook newsfeed on my bed, I clicked on a video that hinted at some happiness or joy. I lucked out, and had such a huge smile on my face for four minutes that the back of my ears hurt. It was wonderful watching this couple of complete strangers dancing at their wedding. The crowd was hooting and cheering, and I felt like I was celebrating too!

A few minutes of scrolling later, after clicking the like button on dog and baby photos, I noticed another video, posted by the same friend, with some heartwarming words in the caption. I clicked on it, and within ninety seconds I had sadness welling up from my belly to my eyes. I felt pressure in my neck and ears, which happens when I bottle up tears.

I thought about it for a second: Do I want to cry now? Do I want my mood to shift from the joy of just a few minutes ago to heartbreaking sorrow?

Even though the video would be hopeful and joyous in a deep way, did I want to be there right now? It took a split second for me to close my heart. I stopped the video and physically changed my environment by stepping into the shower. It was time for a shower anyway, as I was getting ready to go to the airport to start an adventure.

I put the second video out of my mind by thinking of the first video again—it was that easy to change the channel.

There was another consideration in all this too, that of how my mood would affect my husband. Did I want to show up to him as an emotional mess at the start of a vacation? Moods are contagious, and I didn't want the curtain to close on the show!

And there is some discernment here I want to tease out. The videos raising and lowering my mood were not personal. They were not my life; they did not involve people known to me; I did not need to take it in. If a friend or loved one was suffering, it wouldn't be so easy to change the channel.

There is a lesson here that bears illuminating: often *we have a choice* as to what information we allow into our eyes, ears, and hearts.

Protect your heart this month and every other month of the year. Choose wisely.

CLEAR A PATH

Clear a path,

Settle,

Allow your thoughts to drift down;

Gently sweep them aside with a soft broom,
the kind that looks handmade from natural
grasses.

Some of the little notes now in piles on the
perimeter of your awareness are things to
return to later—not now, but later—so you
keep them safe.

Other notes are best to release—the worry, the
rumination that woke you at 4 a.m.
Go ahead and toss that sticky stack into the small
round fire bowl,
The smoke swirling as that which does not serve
you dematerializes.

Settle your mind to clear a path to your heart
where joy and suffering slosh;

Your heart, which when broken, miraculously
goes on beating;

Your heart safety valves, allowing your mind to crank the hatches shut when too much suffering threatens to drop you to the inky bottom of the sea.

You can open the hatch a peep,
Feeling into whether it's OK right now to let tears move through you.

Too much? Crank it down to steer your mind to translucent waters;

That's skillful maneuvering,

Turning your attention toward joy in that moment,
Noticing beauty out the window,
Letting a song stir your soul,
Enjoying the perfect cup of tea,
Relishing the sound of your friend's voice on the phone,

Or my favorite, the sound of my voice in my head, calling myself sweetheart and letting me know that this too shall pass, both the good and the bad, in waves of beginnings and endings.

DEPRESSION AND MINDFULNESS: KEEPING IT REAL

At different stages of my life, I have suffered with depression. The first time was after the birth of my first child. Mindfulness helped me heal from postpartum depression.

I have this memory from 1990 of feeling like my little baby and I were all alone in the universe. The love I felt for him was heartbreaking. I could sit and watch him sleep for hours, waiting for his little cherub lip to quiver in his slumber. Everything else in my life felt too bright, too loud, too something ... too raw. My body was a disaster, and my mind wasn't too far behind. The only bright spot was the baby.

I had flashbacks of giving birth for months. It was terrifying and excruciating.

They call it a precipitous delivery, when your cervix dilates from four to ten centimeters in less than ten minutes. His head was stuck behind my tailbone, and they were pushing so hard on my back it felt like it broke. The anesthesiologist wouldn't give me an epidural because they didn't have an IV running. She responded to my screams for drugs with "You're not getting any drugs, honey; your baby is coming out now." It felt like someone was cutting my body open with an axe and pulling out my organs— and that was a vaginal delivery!

I didn't realize that the flashbacks and feelings of isolation and sadness were classic postpartum depression. I thought it was not postpartum depression because I didn't have feelings of wanting to harm the baby. I figured I was just a little screwed up, and that maybe I wasn't emotionally equipped to be a mom.

Four years later, after surviving a hemorrhage during the delivery of identical twin girls and eighteen weeks of bed rest, I knew how to recognize postpartum depression when it hit me like a wave and tumbled me to the bottom of the sea. I stabilized after finding the right antidepressant and enlisting the help of a wonderful psychotherapist, but it wasn't until I studied mindfulness that I turned the stress in my life around.

I healed myself, rewired my brain, and now, as a mindful self-compassion teacher, I help others to do the same.

IF YOU ARE STRUGGLING TO GET THROUGH THE DAY, TRY SNAP

Soothing touch: Use gentle touch. Place your hands lovingly on your cheeks, over your heart, on your shoulders, or anywhere that you find comforting. This supportive and gentle touch activates our mammalian caregiver response and provides real comfort.

Name the emotion: Oh, that's sadness, that's being overwhelmed, that's hopelessness, that's fear.

Act: Do what brings you joy. Make a joy list, then choose one or more things from it each day. Give yourself this daily gift.

Praise: Tell yourself what you most need to hear. Speak lovingly to yourself. Call yourself "sweetheart" or some other endearing term that feels good to you. Remind yourself that you are loved and capable, and that you are not alone (people all over the world have gone through this).

Later in life, when my kids were teens, depression swamped me again. This time I had mindful self-compassion to help me navigate and heal.

This life can be excruciating.

It can be especially painful for people who are sensitive. We feel a whole world of human suffering at a very visceral level. Watching the news can be incredibly traumatic. (I don't do this anymore. I read or listen to my news.) Then, on top of what often feels like the weight of the world on our shoulders, we have everyday battles, such as tough family situations or health challenges.

It can sometimes be difficult to get through the day.

The reason I now teach and advocate mindfulness tools for soothing yourself when you feel sad, upset, angry, or alone is because these tools are what I used to heal myself. That's how I know they work. I needed this stuff to heal *me*.

Mindfulness doesn't work in a vacuum.

You have to practice it even when you don't need it so you can use it when you need it most. It's not a substitute for therapy, and it's not a substitute for medicine, if you need it. However, thanks to mindfulness, I'm a happy, healthy person who sometimes gets a wave of "Wow, life is tough. This being human stuff is not for cowards," and then I do something to make myself feel better.

I don't need to reach for a cocktail. I don't need to reach for a pill. I now have tools at my disposal, and I help others learn how to do this.

UNBUCKLE

This morning as I lay in bed, I heard from my
    left hip flexor; it had a high-pitched tone, too
    tightly strung.
Then my right ankle joined the song;
Then my left toe.
I rolled onto my belly and imagined unbuckling
my hips,

Unbuckling my ankles;

Dragging my arms down to my sides, I unbuckled
my shoulders.

"Has anyone ever written about unbuckling the
heart," I wondered?

Unbuckling the heart,
Letting the disappointment flow out of the
chambers.

The sadness and grief tucked into the mitral valve
    might need a little scraping to flush it out;

The existential angst at all that is lost every day
in our human family,
That blows away in places like Kentucky and the
Philippines this time;
Next time some other village or town will lose to
nature—our blue marble, in danger, making
itself known again and again.
After the heart is unbuckled and drained into
the river, there is room for the packages to
arrive—
Precious squares of moments intentionally
wrapped and delivered to you, from the
person that knows you best.

Unwrap the smile you remember in a child's eyes;
Unwrap the light flashing on the water;
Unwrap the wind blowing through the mountain
trees;
Unwrap your unique pearls of awe;

Unwrap the truth that love resides here.

Shine your light, sweetheart,
Because shame thrives in the dark.

DON'T ASK ME

Don't ask me how I am;
As sorrow flows through me,
Don't ask me.

If your ears must close to the truth,
Don't ask me.

If your heart must harden to the pain,
Don't ask me.

If your hands hang useless at the end of your limp
arms,
Don't ask me.

When your arms become animated and pulse
with energy, pulling me in for a warm embrace,
I'll know I've been seen.

When your heart softens and shares my sorrow,
I'll know I've been felt.

When your ears open to my quivering voice,
I'll know I've been heard.

Then go ahead,
Ask me how I am.

MINDFUL METHODS TOOLBOX

When paying attention to what you are doing when doing it instead of ruminating on the past or worrying about the future, you are giving your brain a much-needed break. We primates are hardwired to worry and ruminate, but we need to reset after perceived danger to get back to our baseline, which is a calm state, often called the tend-and-befriend state. This allows the cortisol and adrenaline that helped us react to danger to dissipate. If we stay in the danger zone, the cortisol and adrenaline that kicks in to help us fight, flight, or freeze can wear us down and make us sick. All the tools in the Mindful Methods Toolbox are techniques to help us get home to our true nature—calm and open with loving awareness. Please use this list as a reference, noting what tools work for you in which situations. Use your creativity to add to the list!

In the stories in this book, you saw how these tools are applied in various situations to manage difficult emotions. Finding what techniques work each time is trial and error, which is part of the practice. Eventually, you might have a favorite dozen, like I do. The first two are foundational to SNAP—soothing touch and naming the emotion.

1. Soothing touch. Place your hands on your heart, face, arms, belly, or hand in hand to find your soothing touch place. The release of oxytocin and endorphins will help calm your nervous system.
2. Name the emotion. Name it to tame it so that you can feel it to heal it. Naming the emotion engages your thinking brain to help you calm down when you are feeling overwhelmed. After naming the emotion, you can

apply one of the many appropriate mindful methods to help you feel better.

3. Joy list. Write a list of all the things that bring you joy; keep your joy list handy!

4. Meditate every day. Download the Insight Timer app and the *Balanced Mind with Julie Potiker* podcast for free guided meditations. Check out the Calm app or the Headspace app.

5. Ask yourself, "What do I need to hear right now?"

6. Ask yourself, "What do I need to do right now?"

7. Ground yourself by dropping your attention to the soles of your feet. How do they feel? Warm or cold? Moist or dry?

8. Ground yourself by using a here-and-now stone, rosary, or mala. Focus your attention on the temperature and texture of the object.

9. Connect with other humans. Try to see someone who cares about you on Zoom or FaceTime if seeing them in person isn't feasible. A phone call might be enough, or even a comforting text exchange.

10. Bring to mind people who care about you and people you care about to help you feel loved and safe.

11. Practice calling yourself "sweetheart" or another term of endearment.

12. Practice mindfulness while brushing your teeth. Close your eyes and feel and taste the experience.

13. Practice mindful cooking. Focus on the colors, textures, and aromas of the experience.

14. Practice mindful eating. Before you slowly take your first bite, consider the journey the ingredients took, from being harvested to making their way to your kitchen. Feel gratitude for all the hands that made that happen.

15. Practice mindful walking. Open up your senses to the sights, sounds, temperature, smells—everything you can notice.

16. Practice taking in the good any time you notice a positive mental state, letting it land for a few breaths so you push the good mental state to a neural trait. (Thanks to Rick Hanson for this simple yet profound practice!)

17. Practice letting music help you be in the moment. Make a playlist of songs that move you.

18. Journal or write.

19. Get out to see things enduring—the sky, trees, water, mountains if nearby, etc. Even looking out the window can help shift your mood and open your perspective.

20. Move your body—walk, stretch, exercise.

21. Practice tonglen, the sending-receiving meditation. Instruction can be found on Insight Timer by searching my name, or search "tonglen" and experience many teachers teaching this ancient practice. I also have tonglen on the *Balanced Mind with Julie Potiker* podcast.

22. Practice loving kindness meditation for yourself and others. Search for either "loving kindness meditation" or "metta meditation" on Insight Timer or the *Balanced Mind with Julie Potiker* podcast. I have over a dozen versions of loving kindness meditations on both apps.

23. Get enough rest and sleep—guided meditations can help. I recommend Kenneth Soares on Insight Timer for guided meditations for sleep.

24. Keep a gratitude practice. The positive feedback loop will make you happier.

25. Be of service, in any way possible. Reach out and call someone you know is alone. Give time or donate to organizations that feed and protect the vulnerable among us. This will benefit you with longer lasting eudaemonic joy as you help others.

EPILOGUE

WORKING WITH AND BEING WITH ...

Driving home the other day I had an impulse, with a voice that whispered, "I could drive right off that cliff." Immediately my head shook. "No, that's ridiculous, I have no intention of doing that! Where did that even come from?"

A few minutes later, I noticed an urge to drive to a dark bar in the afternoon and sit with a double old-fashioned. Wow, that is not happening! I have no interest or intention of doing that either.

That's when my right hand went to my heart (my left hand was on the wheel), and I said, "Oh, Julie, sweetheart, you are suffering. I'm so sorry this is so tough. I'm here for you."

There is a delicate balance between being with your emotions and working with your emotions. We need both. We need to be with what is really there, not to run from it, numb it, or push it down; we need to hold it gently.

Can we see what is real and cultivate a practice that can hold it all?

I think I'm doing it. I think I have a clear mind and an open heart; my practice can hold it all. Suddenly, I got this insight: I'm working through my toolbox like addicts work through the

Twelve Steps. I'm thinking and doing; it's all cognitive. What is happening in my body?

The driving off a cliff or hiding in a bar with booze impulses were messages from my body to my mind. Those stories were my old way of coping with parenting trauma (not that I ever actually drove off a cliff, but I fantasized about doing that, and worse). This new difficulty triggers that old trauma.

This past week I have doubled down on my practice—meditating, exercising, teaching, writing, swimming, watching entertaining TV, reading excellent prose and poetry, contacting my therapist, setting an appointment with my mentor, and keeping the gratitude practice—all in the service of staying afloat. These activities are the hit parade of my toolbox.

I'm wondering whether it's too much "working with" and not enough "being with"?

I once asked Jack Kornfeld how long you are supposed to sit with your bad feelings before helping yourself shift. His answer, "Not too long!" After that, I made it a practice to ask every senior teacher the same question. I got variations on the same answer.

This afternoon, paddling around in the swimming pool (using two of my tools for well-being), I was listening to the Science & Wisdom of Emotions Summit (another tool for well-being) and I heard Resmaa Menakem say we shouldn't call toolboxes "toolboxes." Tools are for fixing things, and when you close your eyes and someone says "tools" your body doesn't feel expansive. If, however, you close your eyes and someone says "toys," your body has a lighter, maybe more wonderous, reaction. He suggests that we change the name to "toy box." I'll contemplate that for a while, but I don't think it will work for me. My tools save my life. I think of toys as mere playthings, more like hedonistic joys. My tools have been forged through fire and honed these last twelve years. These tools are my spears, shields, and hammers. These tools are also my blankets, mugs, and hugs.

I don't have the answer to whether it's too much "working with" and not enough "being with" what is real. I'm just staying afloat, riding the wave of the question.

THE PATH IS THE PRACTICE

The house next to ours was being renovated. What I really mean is that the house next to us was being demolished, slowly, bit by bit. There was a lot of heavy machinery, tools, and, some days, a lot of men. Oh, and a transistor radio.

One morning my husband shuffled into the kitchen and said, "How can you sit there at the table having your coffee with all that racket?"

"It's white noise," I said.

I had decided a month before what my relationship was going to be with the reality of the situation. I could choose to get aggravated and annoyed with the disruption of my peaceful enjoyment of my environment, or I could intentionally decide to not let it bother me. It's possible the noise is going to last for a year, or two … maybe more.

Lately I've noticed lots of earth, some rough old wood-framing that you can see right through, a construction fence that sometimes falls down, and no human beings.

I'm cool with it.

You might think that it's only possible to use these practices, intentionally choosing a mindset, while you are relaxing at home. On the contrary, I think they are even more important when you are out and about living your life.

Yesterday I made a stupid mistake driving, which angered another motorist. He rolled down his window and shouted at me. He was waiting up ahead for me, and when I stopped at the light next to him, I lowered my window to apologize.

He started screaming, "There was a turn lane. You could have hit me! Why did you do that?"

I said, "Listen, you need to take a breath. I said I'm sorry. My nav system told me to turn, and I got flustered and made a mistake. I'm glad you were paying attention and that I didn't hit you. I was wrong, and you were right. I am wrong and you are right. Again, I'm sorry."

He said, "OK, OK, OK, OK," each "OK" deflating his rage. Then he said, "Thank you."

After I drove away, I noticed how rattled I was, and I started crying.

Automatically, I practiced SNAP.

Soothing touch: One hand on my heart, one hand on the wheel!

Name the emotion: "Wow, I'm upset," I said to myself, labeling the emotion.

Act: "It's OK, honey," I said. Then, gently investigating why I got so reactive, I acknowledged to myself that I strongly dislike getting yelled at. Who does? I've never been comfortable with anger, my own anger or someone else's. It brings up old childhood issues and patterns of trauma and survival. I don't need to go there. I've done enough work around those issues!

Praise: I told myself what I needed to hear and what I would like to do to make myself feel better. I told myself that I handled the situation admirably. I owned my screwup. I calmed the situation with the other driver. No one got hurt. Everything was fine. I was safe. Then I took some deep belly breaths, exhaling longer than I inhaled, which slows the heart rate and lowers blood pressure.

After that, I chatted on the phone with one of my older sisters, which made me feel all better.

While taking an online course from Rick Hanson called Neurodharma, I discovered another benefit from regular practice.

It was my third online course with Rick over the past six years. I've also had the privilege of learning with him in person at retreats, trainings, and seminars.

I was happy to note that my practice was getting more solid. Now, when turbulence happens for any reason—whether construction noise that I can't control or daily interpersonal flare-ups—I notice the disturbance, but it doesn't rock my core.

During the Q and A of the first online video, Rick said that as we deepen our keel and as we grow an unshakable core of inner peace, contentment, and love, we recover more quickly from whatever trauma or triggers are hitting us. And it doesn't invade the core of us; it's more like it's on the surface. This explanation makes me think of scuba diving—when you get below the current, it is still.

My practice of SNAP deepens my keel. It enables me to manage difficult emotions so that I stay solid in my deep core, and the surface water smooths down relatively quickly. Rick then took the concept to an existential level when he said that eventually we may increasingly identify as the stream.

Wow, so that's a supercool goal for me!

There was another "ah ha" in the Q and A for me. I've always grappled with the teaching that "we make our own hell by wishing things are different than they are." Because who wouldn't want less suffering in the myriad of situations in our day-to-day lives where suffering occurs? People have medical problems, illness, financial stress, mental health issues, all sorts of suffering in themselves, and they also suffer on behalf of others.

Rick clarified that it's appropriate to want a different outcome, but deep down, being at peace with whatever happens is the key. This is a practice that I will work with for the rest of my life. This isn't about positive thinking. It includes the knowledge of all the crap that is actually going on; but deep down, with practice, maybe it won't eat my heart out!

Honestly, I'm good about 60 percent of the time. Depending on the suffering, I can usually manage to keep it at the surface, let it go, and retain my equanimity.

I feel so fortunate to learn from teachers like Rick who are beckoning us onto the path of healing.

When I ponder the women and men who have been instrumental in my health and my work, it is astounding the breadth and depth of their teachings. Pema Chodrun, Kristin Neff, Tara Brach, Brené Brown, Roshi Joan Halifax, and Michelle Becker have influenced what I teach and how I teach it. Christopher Germer, Rick Hanson, Dan Siegel, Steve Hickman, David Treleaven, and Paul Gilbert are integral to my work.

Relative newcomers Emma Seppälä and Alex Korb are adding their brilliance to the body of work by applying the science of happiness to accelerate your success, as in the case of Emma's book *The Happiness Track*. And Alex's book *The Upward Spiral* is about using neuroscience to reverse the course of depression.

Currently, I'm reading a new book called *Wholehearted* by Koshin Paley Ellison. It's fabulous. He is a Jewish, gay, Zen monk and a psychotherapist. I can see him up ahead on the path, enticing me to join him.

I'm on the path, with one hand reaching to those who came before me, and one hand reaching to you to join me.

May you be safe, happy, healthy, and live with ease.

SPACE

Dust rings,
Gaps,
Torque,
Gravitational pull;
Two trillion galaxies,
Two hundred billion trillion stars,
Red, white, and blue—
Smaller to bigger,
Cooler to hotter,
Farther to closer;
Black holes colliding,
Making a sound,
And me,
Orbiting others;
Attracting,
Repelling,
Spinning,
Standing still;
Smaller to bigger,
Cooler to hotter,
Closer to farther,
Making a sound;
A speck of dust—
Star dust.

INDEX

"Parenting Haiku Style," 113
philanthropy, benefits of, 147
podcasts. *See Balanced Mind with
    Julie Potiker* (podcast)
political strife and disaster, SNAP
    for, 119–149
positive action, taking of, 142–143
Powers, Richard, 24
praise (P in SNAP)
    author's use of after driving
        incident, 181
    for baby safety, 117
    for caregivers, 158
    for dealing with anger, 4
    for dealing with anxiety, 10, 62
    for dealing with contagious
        anxiety, 22
    for dealing with disaster, 154
    for dealing with grief, 47
    for dealing with grief at losing a
        pet, 65–66
    for dealing with grief caused
        by sensitivity to global
        events, 53
    for dealing with medical
        anxiety, 20
    for dealing with personal grief
        triggered by global
        events, 57
    for dealing with political strife
        and disaster, 122–123
    for dealing with weepy waves of
        grief, 74
    for equanimity, 27, 30, 36
    for getting through the
        day, 165
    for help regulating nervous
        system, 76

for inner critic talk on
    appearance, 100
for inner critic work, 92–93
for managing the news, 144
for parenting, 106, 111
for snapping out of
    reactivity, 130
Psychoneuroendrocrinology (journal),
    on stress hormones, 1

R

Ragan, Lyn, 72
RAIN (recognize, allow, investigate
    and non-identification), x
Rainer, Jackson, 68
reactivity, SNAP for, 129–136
"Reflections on 365 Days of Sorrow
    and Healing," 66–69
"Relieving Anxiety and Feeling
    Grounded" (guided
    meditation), 63
"Remembering My Mother on Yom
    Kippur," 70
resilience, 25, 26
rosary, use of, 173

S

S in SNAP (soothing touch). *See*
    soothing touch (S in SNAP)
sadness, SNAP for, 155
Schwartz, Richard C., 100
Science & Wisdom of Emotions
    Summit, 178
"The Screaming Child," 28–29
self-care
    author's forms of, 25, 109
    author's practice of, 44

for managing the news, 143
for parenting, 105, 110
for snapping out of
    reactivity, 129
as tool in Mindful Methods
    Toolbox, 172
Southern Poverty Law Center, 143
"Space," 185
Squirrel Hill (Pittsburgh), massacre
    in, 55
Stang, Heather, 41, 43
stress, consequences of, 1, 7–8
stress eating, limiting of, 146
sudden temporary upsurge of grief
    (STUG), 68–69
sugar intake, cautions with, 146
super woman/super mom, fallacy
    of, 91
Surviving Trauma School Earth
    (Baum), 37

T

"Take in the Good" (course),
    80, 146
"Tech and Me," 94–96
threat-defense system, 3
Together Rising, 143
tolerance, window of, 158
tonglen meditation, 41, 43, 174
touch, soothing (S in SNAP). *See*
    soothing touch (S in SNAP)
toy box, use of, 178–179
Trauma-Sensitive Mindfulness
    (course), 44–45
Treleaven, David, 44–45, 158, 183
Trump, Donald, 124, 125, 136

U

"Unbuckle," 167–168
Understory (Powers), 24
The Upward Spiral (Korb), 183

V

Vaillant, George, 53
vitamin D, 4

W

Waldinger, Robert, 53–54
walking, mindful, 174
websites
    chrisgermer.com (website), 42
    HealingDimensions.com
        (website), 36
    MindfulMethodsForLife.com
        (website), xii
    self.compassion.org
        (website), 90
"When Quitting Isn't an Option,"
    107–109
"Where I Am From," 77–78
Wholehearted (Ellison), 183
Williams, Miller, 130–131, 133
window of tolerance, 158
Winfrey, Oprah, 107–108

Y

YouTube, "Confessions of a Jewish
    Mother: How My Son
    Ruined My Life," 80